Science Vocabulary Building

Grades 5–8

BY
SCHYRLET CAMERON AND CAROLYN CRAIG

COPYRIGHT © 2009 Mark Twain Media, Inc.

ISBN 978-1-58037-491-0

Printing No. CD-404110

Mark Twain Media, Inc., Publishers
Distributed by Carson-Dellosa Publishing LLC

Visit us at www.carsondellosa.com

HPS 232106

Table of Contents

Introduction to the Teacher

Science Vocabulary Building is intended to help students learn terms that are important to the content taught in science. The International Reading Association promotes teaching vocabulary to improve comprehension. As a goal, the National Research Council, organized by the National Academy of Science, has established that all students should achieve scientific literacy. An essential aspect of scientific literacy is gaining a greater knowledge of the subject matter associated with physical, life, and earth science. Providing vocabulary instruction is one of the most significant ways a teacher can promote student understanding and academic achievement in science.

As students progress through grades five through eight and beyond, reading science content becomes progressively more problematic. There is a significant increase in the number of words with three or more syllables. Those students who are skillful in reading these multisyllabic words can read for comprehension without the challenge of word pronunciation. Learning to read these words and understand their meanings increases the readability level for all students.

National and state science standards, science textbooks, and Mark Twain Media science publications were reviewed in an effort to identify commonly used science words for each grade level. This book focuses on teaching these high-utility terms. Words are listed in alphabetical order. Each entry provides the learner with pronunciation and syllabication information to help the student with decoding. The entry also provides a definition and uses the word in context to help the students gain an understanding of the meaning of the word.

The teaching strategies described in this book promote differentiated instruction. Vocabulary building activities provide multiple opportunities for students to learn the language of science. Alternative methods of instruction, such as hands-on activities, small group work, games, and journaling target multiple learning styles and help learners at all levels. Teachers may choose to focus on decoding and word meanings for English-language learners and reluctant readers. Challenging activities provide all students with opportunities for extended learning.

The instructional activities found in this book are designed to promote scientific literacy through vocabulary learning. They can be used as stand-alone units or to supplement and enrich the content area. Each section includes:

- **Alphabetized Word List:** a glossary of high-utility science terms with pronunciation and syllabication sections presented in an easy to read and understand format
- **Vocabulary Building Activities:** provide students with multiple opportunities to learn and use the term
- **Vocabulary Games:** provide meaningful reinforcement of new terms
- **Interactive Vocabulary Building Websites:** provide students with enrichment opportunities

Science Vocabulary Building supports the No Child Left Behind (NCLB) Act. The book promotes student knowledge and understanding of science and mathematics concepts through vocabulary building. The activities are designed to strengthen scientific literacy skills and are correlated to the National Science Education Standards (NSES) and the National Council for Teachers of Mathematics Standards (NCTM).

National Standards

National Science Education Standards (NSES)
> National Research Council (1996). National Science Education Standards. Washington, D.C.: National Academy Press.

Science as Inquiry
- Content Standard A: As a result of activities in grades 5–8, all students should develop abilities necessary to do scientific inquiry.

Physical Science
- Content Standard B: As a result of activities in grades 5–8, all students should develop understanding of properties of objects and materials, motions and forces, and transfer of energy.

Life Science
- Content Standard C: As a result of activities in grades 5–8, all students should develop understanding of structure and function in living systems, reproduction and heredity, populations and ecosystems, and diversity and adaptations of organisms.

Earth and Space Science
- Content Standard D: As a result of activities in grades 5–8, all students should develop understanding of the structure of the earth system, earth's history, and earth in the solar system.

National Council for Teachers of Mathematics Standards (NCTM)
> National Council for Teachers of Mathematics (2000). Principles and Standards for School Mathematics. Reston, VA: National Council for Teachers of Mathematics.

Measurement
- In grades 5–8, students should be able to understand measurable attributes of objects and the units, systems, and processes of measurement.
- In grades 5–8, students should be able to apply appropriate techniques, tools, and formulas to determine measurements.

How to Use This Book

Science reading materials present students with new and often difficult words. If students do not know the meaning of a sufficient proportion of the words in the reading material, they may become frustrated and skip important words, which can make understanding the text difficult. Teaching science vocabulary first will help students build an understanding of the concepts to be taught. The Association for Supervision and Curriculum Development and International Reading Association support using a systematic approach to teaching vocabulary.

Strategies

- Focus on the most important words.
- Provide students with a science-rich environment where they see, hear, read, and speak the new vocabulary words multiple times.
- Have students record word meanings, experiment results, and answers to activities in their science journals. This will provide a review resource for the students and an assessment tool for teachers and parents.

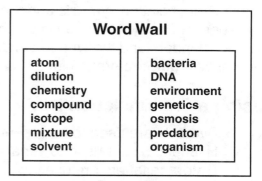

Display words on a bulletin board.

Teaching Science Vocabulary

Step #1–Introduce Words: The teacher reads the word and discusses the information provided in the vocabulary chart.

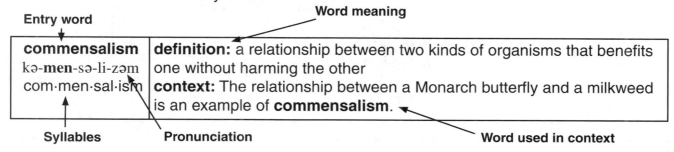

Step #2–Construct Meaning: Students construct their own meaning, write a sentence, and create a visual representation of the word in their science journal.

Word	Definition	Picture
	Sentence	

Step #3–Practice Using the Word: Students gain more knowledge of the words by participating in science activities provided with each word list.

Step #4–Reinforcement: Students participate in a variety of reinforcement activities, such as hangman and charades, to strengthen what they have learned.

Pronunciation Key

What Is a Pronunciation Key?

It is often hard to tell from the spelling of a word how it should be pronounced. A special alphabet of symbols is used to indicate the sounds spoken in the pronunciation of words. A pronunciation key is a list of these symbols and familiar words that contain the sound represented by the symbols.

Pronunciation symbols and their keys differ slightly among various dictionaries and science books. The system used in this book was especially designed to make it easier for you to read and understand the written pronunciations. Place a copy of the key below in your science journal as a quick reference for the pronunciation symbols used in this book.

Using a Pronunciation Key

- Symbols are used to represent the sounds used in the pronunciation of a word.
- Hyphens (-) are used to separate the pronunciations into syllables.
- **Boldface** letters are used to indicate the part of the word to be stressed or spoken with the greatest force.
- In the syllabication listing, dots (·) are used to separate the word into syllables.

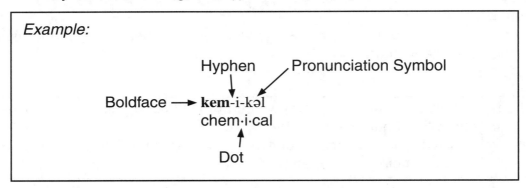

Example:

Hyphen   Pronunciation Symbol

Boldface → **kem**-i-kəl

chem·i·cal

Dot

Pronunciation Key

a	lap, pat, mad	o	hot, top, odd
ā	lane, age, hay	ō	old, toad, know, toe
ä	father, yarn, ah	oi	oil, toy
âr	care, hair	ô	law, caught, for, horse, off, order
e	bet, end, hen, said	o͞o	book, pull, should
ē	bee, equal, piece, real	o͞o	fruit, glue, food, few
ər	better, perfect, baker	ou	out, cow, house
ə	about, taken, pencil, come, circus	sh	she, dish, machine
hw	when, whether, nowhere	th	thin, both
i	kit, in	*th*	this, mother, smooth
ī	ice, my, line, cried	u	cut, up
îr	ear, deer, here, pierce	ûr	fur, term, bird, word, learn

Science Journal

Directions: Complete the vocabulary chart below. Copy the word, make your own definition, write a sentence, and illustrate the word. Collect all your science journal pages in a binder or folder to use as a reference.

Word	Definition	Picture
	Sentence	
Word	Definition	Picture
	Sentence	
Word	Definition	Picture
	Sentence	
Word	Definition	Picture
	Sentence	
Word	Definition	Picture
	Sentence	

Section 1.1: Scientific Method Word List

analyze a-nə-līz an·a·lyze	**definition:** to organize and examine data using narratives, charts, graphs, or tables **context:** After an experiment, a scientist will **analyze** the data to decide what it means.
bias bī-əs bi·as	**definition:** a flaw in the experiment or data analysis that leads to incorrect results **context:** Scientists try to prevent **bias** in their experiments.
classify kla-sə-fī clas·si·fy	**definition:** to use a system to group information into categories **context:** Scientists can **classify** all things into two groups: living and nonliving.
compare kəm-**per** com·pare	**definition:** to examine and notice the similarities or differences **context:** The student will **compare** the similarities in data from the two experiments.
conclusion kən-**klōō**-zhən con·clu·sion	**definition:** the last part of an experiment where the findings are summarized **context:** The student summarized the results of his experiment in the **conclusion**.
constant **kän**-stənt con·stant	**definition:** a factor in an experiment that does not change **context:** The **constant** in the experiment was watering the plant every day at noon.
control group kən-**trōl** grōōp con·trol group	**definition:** the subjects in an experiment that do not get the independent variable **context:** The **control group** of plants received no fertilizer.
data **dā**-tə da·ta	**definition:** a group of measurements, facts, or statistics recorded about an experiment **context:** She graphed the **data** from the rock lab.
dependent variable di-**pen**-dənt **ver**-ē-ə-bəl de·pen·dent var·i·a·ble	**definition:** the factor that changes as a result of the independent variable in an experiment **context:** The **dependent variable** was the increase in the height of the plant as a result of being fertilized.
examine ig-**za**-mən ex·am·ine	**definition:** to look closely at someone or something **context:** **Examine** a small amount of sand under a low-powered microscope.
experiment ik-**sper**-ə-mənt ex·per·i·ment	**definition:** the steps used to test a hypothesis **context:** The student designed an **experiment** to test his hypothesis.
formulate **fòr**-myə-lāt for·mu·late	**definition:** to form an idea about the results of an experiment **context:** The student will analyze the data and **formulate** a conclusion.

Section 1.1: Scientific Method Word List (cont.)

hypothesis hī-**pä**-thə-səs hy·poth·e·sis	**definition:** an idea about the solution to a problem that can be tested or investigated **context:** He designed an experiment to test his **hypothesis**.
identify ī-**den**-tə-fī i·den·ti·fy	**definition:** to name or recognize a person, place, or thing **context:** The student will **identify** the colors in a rainbow.
independent variable in-də-**pen**-dənt **ver**-ē-ə-bəl in·de·pen·dent var·i·a·ble	**definition:** the one factor changed by the person doing the experiment **context:** The **independent variable** was the addition of a time-released fertilizer to the experimental group.
infer in-**fər** in·fer	**definition:** to make an interpretation or conclusion based on reasoning to explain an observation **context:** From the science fair project, it was easy to **infer** that the student had learned a great deal about magnets.
measure **me**-zhər mea·sure	**definition:** to assign numbers to an observation such as length, mass, or volume **context:** **Measure** the length of your desk to the nearest centimeter.
observe əb-**zərv** ob·serve	**definition:** to use the senses to gather information about an object or event **context:** **Observe** what the wind does to leaves, twigs, and other debris on the ground.
predict pri-**dikt** pre·dict	**definition:** a forecast of future events based on previous observations and experiments **context:** Using the data from the experiment, he could **predict** which patients were at risk of having a heart attack.
procedure prə-**sē**-jər pro·ce·dure	**definition:** a set of steps to follow to perform a specific task **context:** The science teacher displayed the **procedure** to follow for the experiment.
record ri-**kȯrd** re·cord	**definition:** to create an account of information for later use **context:** The scientist will **record** the data on a table.
research ri-**sərch** re·search	**definition:** the method of collecting information and data about a topic being studied **context:** The students used their **research** to write a report.
scientific method sī-ən-ti-fik **me**-thəd sci·en·tif·ic me·thod	**definition:** a series of steps scientists use to solve a problem **context:** Students follow the **scientific method** when creating a science fair project.
variable **ver**-ē-ə-bəl var·i·a·ble	**definition:** one of the factors in an experiment **context:** Identify the **variables** in your experiment.

Section 1.1: Vocabulary Building Activities

Scientific Method: Below is a diagram of the scientific method. Copy the diagram in your science journal and fill in the missing explanations for each step.

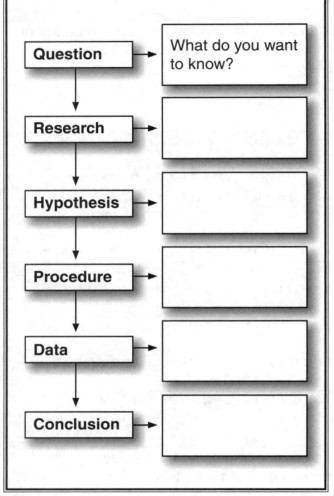

Variables: When testing a hypothesis, you need two groups:

- the experimental group in which you only change one variable at a time
- the control group in which there are no variables

For each hypothesis below, name the variable that would be changed to help prove the hypothesis and the controlled variables that would stay the same for every test.

<u>Hypothesis #1</u>: Flashlights last longer with "Ever Last" brand batteries.

Variable: _____

_____

Control Group: _____

_____

_____

<u>Hypothesis #2</u>: Plants grow taller when given fertilizer.

Variable: _____

_____

Control Group: _____

_____

_____

Formulate a Conclusion: The concluding statement will either support or not support your original hypothesis.

Read the hypothesis and analyze the data below. On your own paper, write a conclusion for the scientific investigation.

<u>Hypothesis</u>: Flashlights run longer with "Ever Last" batteries.

Test Results

Brand	Starting Time	Stopping Time	Hours of Operation
Ever Last	5:00 P.M.	11:00 A.M.	18 hours
Mighty Power	5:00 P.M.	11:00 P.M.	6 hours
#1 Battery	5:00 P.M.	7:00 P.M.	2 hours

Section 1.1: Vocabulary Building Activities (cont.)

The Big Question: Scientists ask questions about what they see going on in their world. They explain exactly what they want to learn from the scientific investigation by writing a question, called the "Big Question." After they have written the "Big Question," scientists predict what they will find out. Scientists call this careful guess a hypothesis.

Practice writing a "Big Question" and hypothesis for each topic. Some boxes have been completed for you.

Topic	Question	Hypothesis
white bread mold		Bread mold does not need light for reproduction on white bread.
paper towels		
plants		Plants grow taller and stronger when given fertilizer.
conserving water	Does washing dishes by hand use less water than an electric dishwasher?	
magnets		

Variables—Identify the variables:

Example:

Question: Does heating a cup of water allow it to dissolve more sugar?

Independent Variable: temperature of the water measured in degrees Celsius

Dependent Variable: amount of sugar that dissolves completely measured in grams

Controlled Variables: stirring, type of sugar, amount of water

Try (Identify the variables in your scientific journal):

Question: How fast does a candle burn?

Independent Variable:

Dependent Variable:

Controlled Variables:

Steps in the Scientific Method: Put the steps to the scientific method in order by numbering 1 through 6.

Step #_____ Draw Conclusions

Step #_____ Research the Problem

Step #_____ Analyze the Data

Step #_____ Design and Carry Out the Experiment

Step #_____ Choose a Problem

Step #_____ Construct a Hypothesis

Online Resource: Use games and puzzles to learn more about the scientific method at the website below.

"Kids DO Science: fun and games." The University of Georgia. < http://www.uga.edu/srel/kidsdoscience/kidsdoscience-fun.htm >

Section 1.2: Scientific Equipment Word List

beaker bē-kər bea·ker	**definition:** glass container used to hold liquids **context:** The student used the **beaker** to hold liquid for an experiment.	
Bunsen burner bən-sən bər-nər bun·sen bur·ner	**definition:** used for heating, sterilization, and combustion **context:** The flame on a **Bunsen burner** can be regulated by changing the air and gas mixture.	
Buret clamp byŏŏ-**ret klamp** bu·ret clamp	**definition:** used to hold apparatus, may be fastened to a ring stand **context:** The scientist fastened the **Buret clamp** to the ring stand.	
ceramic fiber square sə-**ra**-mik fī-bər **skwer** ce·ram·ic fi·ber square	**definition:** used under hot apparatus to protect tables **context:** Place the heated flask on the **ceramic fiber square** to protect the table top.	
chemical spoon ke-mi-kəl **spŏŏn** chem·i·cal spoon	**definition:** used to transfer solids **context:** The student used a **chemical spoon** to transfer salt to the beaker.	
coverslip kə-vər-slip cov·er·slip	**definition:** used to cover objects placed on a slide **context:** Place the **coverslip** over the drop of pond water to slow evaporation from the surface of the slide.	
crucible krŏŏ-sə-bəl cru·ci·ble	**definition:** a vessel used to heat small amounts of solids **context:** Chemical compounds are placed in a **crucible** before heating to very high temperatures.	
Erlenmeyer flask ər-lən-mī-ər **flask** Er·len·mey·er flask	**definition:** used to contain reaction solutions, may be heated **context:** The shape of the **Erlenmeyer flask** allows the contents to be swirled without danger of spilling.	
evaporating dish i-**va**-pə-rāt-ing **dish** evap·o·rat·ing dish	**definition:** used to recover dissolved solids by evaporation **context:** Heat a small amount of salt water in an **evaporating dish** and see what happens.	
Florence flask flȯr-əns **flask** Flor·ence flask	**definition:** used to contain reaction solutions, may be heated **context:** The rounded bottom of the **Florence flask** makes it ideal for boiling liquids.	
forceps fȯr-səps for·ceps	**definition:** used to pick up small objects **context:** The scientist used the **forceps** to hold the cotton thread over the flame of the Bunsen burner.	
funnel fən-l fun·nel	**definition:** used to pour liquid **context:** The student used the **funnel** to channel the water into the flask.	

Section 1.2: Scientific Equipment Word List (cont.)

graduated cylinder **gra**-jə-wāt-ed **si**-lən-dər grad·u·at·ed cyl·in·der	**definition:** used to make accurate measurements of liquid volumes **context:** Measure 10 milliliters of water in a **graduated cylinder**.	
iron ring **ī**-ərn **ring** iron ring	**definition:** used to support apparatus on a ring stand **context:** The student fastened the **iron ring** to the ring stand to support the flask during the experiment.	
magnet **mag**-nət mag·net	**definition:** used to attract or repel other objects made of iron or steel **context:** Use the **magnet** to pick up the iron filings.	
medicine dropper **me**-də-sən **drä**-pər med·i·cine drop·per	**definition:** used to transfer small amounts of liquid **context:** Use the **medicine dropper** to add two drops of iodine to the test tube.	
microscope **mī**-krə-skōp mi·cro·scope	**definition:** used for viewing objects that are too small to be seen by the naked eye **context:** Use the **microscope** to observe the microorganisms in the pond water.	
microscope slide **mī**-krə-skōp **slīd** mi·cro·scope slide	**definition:** narrow piece of glass used as a platform for viewing objects under the microscope **context:** The teacher used lens paper to clean the **microscope slide**.	
mortar and pestle **mor**-tər and **pe**-səl mor·tar and pes·tle	**definition:** used to grind solids into powders **context:** Place the charcoal in the **mortar** and grind it to a fine powder with the **pestle**.	
pinch clamp **pinch klamp** pinch clamp	**definition:** used to connect equipment **context:** Use the **pinch clamp** to fasten the rubber connector to the Bunsen burner.	
pipestem triangle **pīp**-stem **trī**-ang-gəl pipe·stem tri·an·gle	**definition:** used to support a crucible **context:** The scientist placed a **pipestem triangle** on an iron ring to provide a stage for a crucible.	
pipet pī-**pet** pi·pet	**definition:** used to make exact volume measurements of liquids **context:** The student used a **pipet** to place 2 mL of water in the flask.	
ring stand **ring stand** ring stand	**definition:** used to support other apparatus **context:** The student used the **ring stand** to hold a flask during the experiment.	
rubber connector rə-bər kə-**nek**-tər rub·ber con·nec·tor	**definition:** used to connect parts of apparatus **context:** Attach the **rubber connector** to the gas supply for the Bunsen burner.	
safety eyewear **sāf**-tē **ī**-wer safe·ty eye·wear	**definition:** used to prevent injury to the eye **context:** The teacher instructed the students to put on their **safety eyewear** before doing the lab work.	

Section 1.2: Scientific Equipment Word List (cont.)

spatula spa-chə-lə spat·u·la	**definition:** used to transfer solid chemicals in weighing **context:** The **spatula** is used like a spoon to transfer powder to the test tube.	
spring scale spring skāl spring scale	**definition:** used to measure mass or force **context:** Use a **spring scale** to measure the amount of force needed to pull the brick across the table.	
stoppers stä-pərs stop·pers	**definition:** used to close the openings of flasks or test tubes **context:** A **stopper** was placed in the opening of the test tube to seal out airborne contaminants.	
support ring sə-**port ring** sup·port ring	**definition:** used to support glassware, attached to a ring stand **context:** Fasten the **support ring** to the ring stand to hold the beaker.	
10-centimeter ruler 10 **sen**-tə-**mē**-tər **rü**-lər 10 cen·ti·me·ter rul·er	**definition:** used to measure length **context:** The **10-centimeter ruler** was used to measure the length of the ladybug.	
test tube test tōōb test tube	**definition:** used to hold or heat small amounts of liquid **context:** The student placed two drops of water in each **test tube**.	
test tube holder test tōōb hōl-dər test tube hold·er	**definition:** used to hold test tubes for heating **context:** Grasp the hot test tube with the **test tube holder**.	
test tube rack test tōōb rak test tube rack	**definition:** used to hold several test tubes **context:** A **test tube rack** was used to hold the clean test tubes.	
thermometer thər-**mäm**-ət-ər ther·mom·e·ter	**definition:** used to determine temperature **context:** The student measured the temperature of the liquids using a **thermometer**.	
triple beam balance tri-pəl bēm bal-ləns tri·ple beam bal·ance	**definition:** used to measure mass **context:** The **triple beam balance** was used to measure the mass of the apple.	
utility clamp yōō-**ti**-lə-tē **klamp** u·til·i·ty clamp	**definition:** used to hold a test tube, attached to a ring stand **context:** Adjust the **utility clamp** holding the test tube.	
wash bottle wäsh bät-l wash bot·tle	**definition:** used for rinsing solids out of a container when filtering **context:** Fill the **wash bottle** with water and rinse out the test tubes.	
watch glass wäch glas watch glass	**definition:** used to hold very small amounts of liquid **context:** The students were instructed to place a small amount of liquid in the **watch glass**.	

Section 1.2: Vocabulary Building Activities

Science Catalogue Search

Using a science catalogue, locate the following information for the equipment found in the vocabulary list. Write the information in your science journal.

1. purpose of the equipment
2. price of the item
3. page number for the location of the information

Graduated Cylinder

Practice measuring volume using a graduated cylinder. Place three graduated cylinders on a table. In one pour 23 mL of liquid, in the next pour 49 mL of liquid, and in the last pour 68 mL of liquid.

Reminder: When measuring liquid volume, you read the measurement from the bottom of the meniscus. The meniscus is the curve formed because of the adhesion of the liquid to the container.

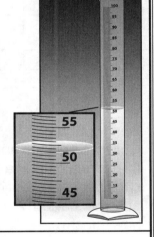

Flask:

Stretch a large, empty balloon over the mouth of a flask. Place the flask on a stand over a Bunsen burner and heat the flask. Observe what happens when you turn the burner off. Explain why the balloon expanded and then contracted with the heating and cooling of the flask. Record observations in your science journal.

Flash Cards:

Create Cards: Start with a stack of blank index cards. Cut the pictures out of the Science Equipment vocabulary pages. On one side of the index card, write the name of one of the pieces of science equipment. On the back of the card, glue the picture of the science equipment.

Review Using Cards: To use the cards effectively, view the picture of the science equipment. Do you know the name of the equipment? Check the back of the card. If you answered correctly, set the card aside. If you were wrong, place the card on the back of your stack so that you will see it again. Proceed through your stack of cards. Set aside cards you get right and continue through cards you get wrong until you have identified all equipment correctly.

Bunsen Burner:

Use the diagram to identify the parts of the Bunsen burner. Write the answers in your science journal.

A. base
B. air ports
C. barrel
D. gas inlet
E. needle valve

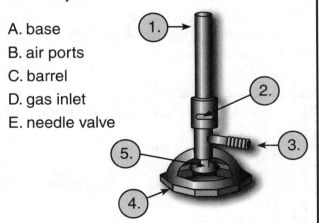

Online Resource:

"Reading a Triple Beam Balance." Wisconsin Technical College. <http://www.wisc-online.com/objects/index_ tj.asp?objID=GCH202>

Section 1.2: Vocabulary Building Activities (cont.)

Safety Eyewear:

Put on your safety eyewear. Light a candle. Take a piece of cotton thread and hold one end of it with the forceps. Hold the thread over the candle. Watch how it burns. Repeat the directions for a wool thread. Copy the data table below and record your observations. What color are the ashes, and do they appear powdery or shiny?

Thread	Description of Ashes	
cotton	color	powdery or shiny
wool	color	powdery or shiny

Microscope:

Collect a variety of water samples: pond, river, tap, bottled, rain, and others. Label each sample. Place one drop of water from each sample on separate slides. Place a coverslip over the water. View the water under the microscope. Copy the data table below. Draw any microorganisms present in the water. Use reference books to identify each organism you found in the water sample. Label your drawings with the correct organism name.

Pond Water	River Water
Bottled Water	Tap Water
Rain Water	Other Sample

Medicine Dropper:

Iodine will turn dark purple or black when it comes in contact with substances that contain starch. Divide a sheet of paper into 8 squares. Place a small portion of the following foods in the squares: white bread, cookie, cooked noodle, saltine cracker, cheese, lettuce, cooked rice, and zucchini. Using a medicine dropper, add two drops of iodine to each food sample. Copy the data table below and record your observations.

Food	Contains Starch?
1. bread	Yes/No
2. cookie	Yes/No
3. noodles	Yes/No
4. cracker	Yes/No
5. cheese	Yes/No
6. lettuce	Yes/No
7. rice	Yes/No
8. zucchini	Yes/No

Spring Scale:

Collect and clean an empty milk carton from the school cafeteria. Tie a string around the carton and connect it to a spring scale. First, pull the carton across the table. Record how much force it took to move the box. Force is measured in newtons (N). Next, fill the carton with marbles. Use the spring scale to pull the carton across the table. Copy the data table below. Record the amount of force used to pull the empty carton and the full carton.

Carton	Force in Newtons
empty carton	
full carton	

Section 1.2: Vocabulary Building Activities (cont.)

Thermometer:

Pour cold water into one cup and hot water into the other. Place thermometers with the Fahrenheit, Celsius, and Kelvin scale in each cup. Copy the data table below. Record the temperature of the liquid in each cup after 4 minutes.

	Fahrenheit	Celsius	Kelvin
cold			
hot			

Test Tube:

Discover how dish soap works. Add a few drops of cooking oil to a test tube half filled with water. Place a stopper in the opening of the test tube. Shake the tube vigorously. Notice that the oil is broken up into drops that soon come together again. Now add a drop of dish soap, shake the tube again, and notice the drops of oil disappear. The function of soap is to break down oil into fine droplets, forming an emulsion. These droplets can then easily be rinsed away.

10-Centimeter Ruler:

Collect a variety of packaged vegetable seeds from your local garden center. Measure seeds using a 10-centimeter ruler. Copy the table below. Record your measurements to the nearest millimeter.

Seed	Measurement
lettuce	
radish	
carrot	

Triple Beam Balance:

Target Mass	Items Used	Actual Mass
1 gram		
5 grams		
10 grams		
20 grams		
50 grams		
100 grams		

Fill different film canisters with various objects such as pennies, paper clips, popcorn, screws, or washers that will get you closest to the targeted mass. Now, measure the mass of each canister using the triple beam balance scale. Copy the table above and record your data.

Ring Stand:

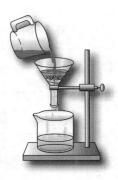

Discover how the earth filters our water supply. Support a large glass funnel on a ring stand over a beaker. Fill the funnel with clean pebbles, coarse sand, and fine sand, as shown in the diagram. Pour some muddy water through this filter unit. Observe the water in the beaker. (Although most of the solid impurities have been removed, the water is still not safe for drinking.)

Online Resource: Knowing the names and uses of laboratory equipment is an important part of science. At this website, you will learn more about lab equipment. "Lab Equipment." ThinkQuest.
<http://www.cartage.org.lb/en/themes/Sciences/Chemistry/Analyticalchemistry/LabEquipment/LabEquipment.htm>

Section 1.3: Scientific Measurement Word List

Words That Describe Measurement

accuracy a-kyə-rə-sē ac·cu·ra·cy	**definition:** to compare a measurement to the actual value of an object **context:** A digital clock enables scientists to measure time with much greater **accuracy** than a sundial.
estimate es-tə-māt es·ti·mate	**definition:** to make an educated guess **context:** The student **estimated** the length of the desk.
measurement me-zhər-mənt mea·sure·ment	**definition:** to communicate information using numbers **context:** Scientists use **measurement** to describe the world.
precision pri-**si**-zhən pre·ci·sion	**definition:** to consistently get the same answer when an item is measured several times **context:** When measuring time, an analog clock and a digital clock provide a different level of **precision**.

The International System (SI) of Measurement

Scientists throughout the world use the SI system of measurement. It is based on the metric system.

Measurement	Definition	SI Unit	Symbol
length	the distance between two points	meter	m
volume	the measure of the amount of space an object occupies	cubic meter	m^3
mass	the measure of the amount of matter in an object	kilogram	kg
weight	the measure of force	newton	N
temperature	the measure of the amount of heat an object has	kelvin	K
time	the measure for the interval between two events	second	s
area	the measure of the number of square units needed to cover the faces or surfaces of a figure	square meters	m^2
electric current	the measure of the rate of flow of electric current	ampere	A
amount of substance	the measure of the molecular weight of a substance	Mole	mol
luminous intensity	the measure of the brightness of a light source	candela	cd
density	the measure of the amount of matter that occupies a particular space	grams per cubic centimeter	g/cm^3

Section 1.3: Scientific Measurement Word List (cont.)

SI Prefixes	
Prefix	**Meaning**
kilo-	1,000
hecto-	100
deca-	10
Unit	1
deci-	0.1
centi-	0.01
milli-	0.001

Using the Prefix Table

Adding a prefix to the unit of measurement changes its value.

Example:
    kilo + meter = 1,000 meters
    hecto + meter = 100 meters
    deci + meter = 0.1 meter
    centi + meter = 0.01 meter
    milli + meter = 0.001 meter

The Metric System is used to measure SI units.

Length	Mass	Capacity
1 millimeter = 0.001 meter	1 milligram = 0.001 gram	1 milliliter = 0.001 liter
1 centimeter = 0.01 meter	1 centigram = 0.01 gram	1 centiliter = 0.01 liter
1 decimeter = 0.1 meter	1 decigram = 0.1 gram	1 deciliter = 0.1 liter
1 kilometer = 1,000 meters	1 kilogram = 1,000 grams	1 kiloliter = 1,000 liters
Abbreviations	**Abbreviations**	**Abbreviations**
1 millimeter = 1 mm	1 milligram = 1 mg	1 milliliter = 1 mL
1 centimeter = 1 cm	1 centigram = 1 cg	1 centiliter = 1 cL
1 meter = 1 m	1 decigram = 1 dg	1 deciliter = 1 dL
1 decimeter = 1 dm	1 gram = 1 g	1 liter = 1 L
1 kilometer = 1 km	1 kilogram = 1 kg	1 kiloliter = 1 kL

Other Measurements Used in Science

Temperature is expressed in degrees (°). The Fahrenheit (°F) and Celsius (°C) temperature scales are the two most common scales used in science classrooms and on thermometers. Most thermometers have both scales. If you know the temperature in one scale, you can read across to tell the temperature in the other scale.

Time:
1 minute = 60 seconds (SI)
1 hour = 60 minutes = 3,600 seconds
1 day = 24 hours   1 week = 7 days
4 weeks = 1 month (approx.)
52 weeks = 1 year   1 year = 365 1/4 days

Thermometers

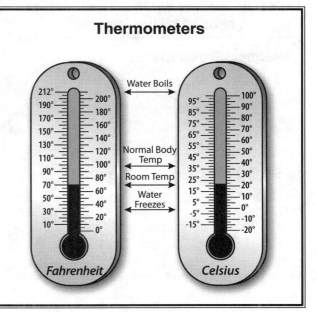

Section 1.3: Vocabulary Building Activities

Conversions

Sometimes scientists need to convert from one unit of measure to another similar unit. Converting from one unit to another involves using mathematical operations. Examine the example problems below, then complete the practice problems on your own paper.

Example Problem 1: How many centimeters are there in 7 meters?	
Step 1: Write down the measurement you want to convert.	7 meters
Step 2: Write the conversion factor for the problem. The conversion factor is written as a fraction.	$7 \text{ m} \times \dfrac{100 \text{ cm}}{1 \text{ m}}$ $\dfrac{\text{units you are converting to}}{\text{units you are converting from}}$
Step 3: The units in the measurement you want to convert cancel out the units in the denominator of the fraction.	$7 \text{ m} \times \dfrac{100 \text{ cm}}{1 \text{ m}}$
Step 4: Multiply the measurement you want to convert by the fraction.	$7 \times \dfrac{100}{1} = \dfrac{700}{1} = 700 \text{ cm}$
Example Problem 2: 50 centimeters equal how many meters?	
Step 1: Write down the measurement you want to convert.	50 centimeters
Step 2: Write the conversion factor for the problem. The conversion factor is written as a fraction.	$50 \text{ cm} \times \dfrac{1 \text{ m}}{100 \text{ cm}}$ units you are converting to / units you are converting from
Step 3: The units in the measurement you want to convert cancel out the units in the denominator of the fraction.	$50 \text{ cm} \times \dfrac{1 \text{ m}}{100 \text{ cm}}$
Step 4: Multiply the measurement you want to convert by the fraction.	$50 \times \dfrac{1}{100} = \dfrac{50}{100} = 0.5 \text{ m}$

Practice Problems:

1. 6 mL = _____ L
2. 48 L = _____ mL
3. 88 kg = _____ g
4. 108 g = _____ kg
5. 12 cm = _____ mm
6. 14 m = _____ cm
7. 6.25 L = _____ mL
8. 9.5 m = _____ cm

Length:

With a partner, measure both your heights in millimeters. Copy the data table below and record your measurements. Now, convert each measurement to centimeters, decimeters, and meters.

Name	mm	cm	dm	m

Section 1.3: Vocabulary Building Activities (cont.)

Length: With a partner, choose five objects in your classroom to measure. Estimate the length and then measure with a meter stick. Copy the table below and record your answers.

Object	Length	
	Estimate	**Measurement**
1.		
2.		
3.		
4.		
5.		

Volume: Pour 50 mL of water into a graduated cylinder. Place a marble in the water.

1. How much space does the marble occupy?
2. If 1 mL of water occupies exactly 1 cm³ of space, what is the volume of the marble in cm³?
3. Find the volume of other objects. Create a table to record your data.

Metric Study Guide:
Fold a sheet of white unlined paper in half like a hotdog bun. Next, fold the paper in fourths and then in eighths. Unfold the paper. You now have a hotdog folded in 8 equal parts. Form 8 tabs by cutting along the folds on one side of the paper. Write important terms on the front tabs. Write definitions and important information under the tabs. Use the foldable to help you study the metric measurement terms.

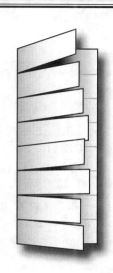

Converting Temperature: This online calculator will let you convert between various temperature measurements. "Temperature Conversion Calculator." ScienceLab. <http://www.sciencelab.com/data/conversion_calculators/temperature-conversion.shtml>

Temperature: Find the temperature in degrees Fahrenheit for 5 cites. The Weather Channel posts the daily temperature for 100 U.S. cities at the website below. Copy the table below and record the temperatures.

Convert the temperatures to Celsius and Kelvin.

City	Fahrenheit (°F)	Celsius (°C) $°C = \dfrac{°F - 32}{1.8}$	Kelvin (°K) $°K = °C + 275$
1.			
2.			
3.			
4.			
5.			

"Top 100." The Weather Channel Interactive, Inc.
<http://www.weather.com/common/drilldown/US/top100.html?from=footer>

Section 2.1: Matter Word List

atom at-əm at·om	**definition:** the smallest part of an element **context:** An **atom** is too small to see, so models are used to explain them.
atomic number ə-**tom**-ik **num**-bər a·tom·ic num·ber	**definition:** the number of protons in the nucleus of each atom of an element **context:** On the periodic table, the elements are listed by **atomic number**.
atomic mass ə-**tom**-ik **mas** a·tom·ic mass	**definition:** the mass of an element; nearly equal to the number of protons and neutrons found in the element's nucleus **context:** The **atomic mass** of sodium is 22.990.
chemical property **kem**-i-kəl **prop**-ər-tē chem·i·cal prop·er·ty	**definition:** a characteristic of a substance that allows it to change to a new substance **context:** A **chemical property** of iron is that it reacts with oxygen in the air and produces rust.
electron i-**lek**-tron e·lec·tron	**definition:** an invisible, negatively charged particle that travels around the nucleus of an atom **context:** **Electrons** orbit the nucleus of an atom.
electron cloud i-**lek**-tron **kloud** e·lec·tron cloud	**definition:** the area surrounding the nucleus of an atom where electrons are likely to be found **context:** The **electron cloud** is made up of the atom's electrons, and it travels in a space around the nucleus.
electron dot diagram i-**lek**-tron **dot** dī-ə-gram e·lec·tron dot di·a·gram	**definition:** the symbol for the element surrounded by as many dots as there are electrons in its outer energy level **context:** The number of electrons in an element's outer energy level is shown by the **electron dot diagram**.
element **el**-ə-mənt el·e·ment	**definition:** a substance made up of only one kind of atom that cannot be divided by ordinary chemical means **context:** Gold is an **element** that cannot be broken down into any other substance by ordinary chemical means.
energy level **en**-ər-jē **lev**-əl en·er·gy lev·el	**definition:** the different positions and specific amount of an electron's energy **context:** **Energy level** refers to the different areas of an atom where electrons are found.
ion **ī**-on i·on	**definition:** an atom that has become electrically charged because it has gained or lost electrons **context:** A negative **ion** atom has more electrons than a positive **ion** atom.
isotopes **ī**-sə-tōps i·so·topes	**definition:** atoms of the same element that have different numbers of neutrons but the same number of protons **context:** Atoms of all **isotopes** of carbon contain the same number of protons, but they do not have the same number of neutrons.

Section 2.1: Matter Word List (cont.)

mass number **mas num**-bər mass num·ber	**definition:** the sum of the number of protons and neutrons in an atom of an element **context:** The number of protons plus the number of neutrons is an element's **mass number**.
matter **măt**-ər mat·ter	**definition:** the term used to describe anything that has mass and takes up space **context:** **Matter** is made up of atoms.
metal **met**-l met·al	**definition:** an element that is malleable, ductile, a good conductor of electricity, and generally has a shiny or metallic luster **context:** Most elements are **metals** and, therefore, will conduct electricity.
metalloid **met**-l-oid met·al·loid	**definition:** an element that has characteristics of both metals and nonmetals and is solid at room temperature **context:** Silicon is a **metalloid** used to make electronic circuits.
molecule **mol**-i-kyo͞ol mol·e·cule	**definition:** the smallest part of a compound that still has the properties of the compound **context:** Water is the most abundant **molecule** on Earth.
neutron **no͞o**-tron neu·tron	**definition:** an uncharged particle located in the nucleus of an atom **context:** The nucleus of an atom is made of two kinds of particles: positively charged protons and neutral **neutrons**.
nonmetal non-**met**-l non·met·al	**definition:** an element that is usually a gas or a brittle solid and is a poor conductor of electricity and heat **context:** The human body is mostly made up of **nonmetals**.
nucleus **no͞o**-klē-əs nu·cle·us	**definition:** the positively charged, central part of an atom **context:** The **nucleus** of an atom is made of two kinds of particles: positively charged protons and neutral neutrons.
periodic table pîr-ē-**od**-ik **tā**-bəl per·i·od·ic ta·ble	**definition:** a chart that organizes the elements by the number of protons in each element's nucleus **context:** A **Periodic Table** contains data about the elements.
physical property **fiz**-i-kəl **prop**-ər-tē phys·i·cal prop·er·ty	**definition:** a characteristic of matter that can be observed, such as color, shape, smell, taste, texture, mass, volume, and density **context:** A **physical property** of clay is that it is malleable; squeezing it changes the shape.
proton **prō**-ton pro·ton	**definition:** a positively charged particle in the nucleus of an atom **context:** **Protons** are located in the nucleus of an atom.
state of matter **stāt** uv **mat**-ər state of mat·ter	**definition:** the physical forms in which a substance can exist: solid, liquid, gas, and plasma **context:** Plasma represents the **state of matter** of the substances in the sun.

Section 2.1: Vocabulary Building Activities

Element Cube: The boxes on the periodic table provide information about the unique properties of each element.

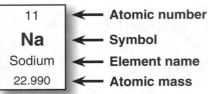

11	← **Atomic number**
Na	← **Symbol**
Sodium	← **Element name**
22.990	← **Atomic mass**

Create a cube for one of the elements on the periodic table. On one face of the cube, copy the information from the Periodic Table about the element you have selected. Research your element and write sentences on the other faces about the element's appearance, properties, and uses.

cut ———
fold - - - - -

Word Shape Puzzles: Decide which words from the vocabulary list fit the word shapes. Write the answers in your science journal.

Example:

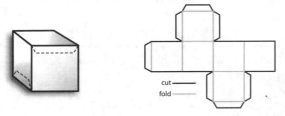

Answer: | a | t | o | m |

1.

2.

Try: Create five word shape puzzles using the matter vocabulary word list. Trade with a partner and solve.

Online Resource: Review the structure of an atom at the following interactive website.
"Build Atoms Yourself." Houghton and Mifflin Company.
<http://www.classzone.com/books/earth_science/terc/content/investigations/es0501/es0501page04.cfm>

Online Resource: Review the basics of the Periodic Table at the following interactive website.
"Atomic Basics: The Periodic Table." Annenberg Media.
<http://www.learner.org/interactives/periodic/basics_5_the_periodic_table.html>

3-D Model of an Atom: Create a 3-dimensional model of an atom that can be hung from a string. Select an element from the list below. Use the periodic table to determine your element's atomic number. Using the information, make a detailed sketch of the atom. Make sure to display the correct number of neutrons, electrons, and protons; these should be in their correct locations. Next, decide what to use to represent the neutrons, elections, and protons. Anything small, round, and that can be glued to each other will work, such as ping-pong balls, small rubber balls, or styrofoam balls. Color-code the balls so that it is easier to identify the protons, neutrons, and electrons. The electrons should be smaller than the protons and neutrons.

Elements:

hydrogen   sodium
carbon   calcium
copper   gold

Section 2.2: Chemistry Word List

catalyst **kat**-l-list cat·a·lyst	**definition:** a material that increases the rate of a chemical reaction by lowering the activation energy **context:** A **catalyst** speeds up a chemical reaction.
chemical bond **kem**-i-kəl **bond** chem·i·cal bond	**definition:** a force that holds two or more atoms together **context:** The atoms of a single water molecule have a **chemical bond**.
chemical equation **kem**-i-kəl i-**kwā**-zhən chem·i·cal e·qua·tion	**definition:** an easy way to show chemical reactions using symbols **context:** $2H_2 + O_2 \rightarrow 2H_2O$ is the **chemical equation** for two molecules of water.
chemical formula **kem**-i-kəl **fôr**-myə-lə chem·i·cal for·mu·la	**definition:** a combination of chemical symbols and numbers that represent the elements in a compound and their proportions **context:** NaCl is the **chemical formula** that represents the compound known as table salt.
chemical reaction **kem**-i-kəl rē-**ak**-shən chem·i·cal re·ac·tion	**definition:** the process in which chemical change occurs, resulting in new substances **context:** When campfire logs burn to ash, this is one example of a **chemical reaction**.
colloid **kol**-oid col·loid	**definition:** a mixture containing small, dissolved particles that do not settle out **context:** Gelatin is an example of a **colloid**.
compound **kom**-pound com·pound	**definition:** a substance made of two or more elements that are combined chemically **context:** Water is a **compound** formed by combining hydrogen and oxygen.
endothermic reaction en-dō-**thûr**-mik rē-**ak**-shən en·do·ther·mic re·ac·tion	**definition:** a reaction in which heat energy is absorbed, cooling the surroundings **context:** Baking bread and frying an egg are examples of **endothermic reactions**.
exothermic reaction ek-sō-**thûr**-mik rē-**ak**-shən ex·o·ther·mic re·ac·tion	**definition:** a chemical reaction in which heat energy is released and causes the temperature of the immediate surroundings to rise **context:** A dynamite explosion is an **exothermic reaction**.
heterogeneous mixture het-ər-ə-jē-nē-əs **miks**-chər het·er·o·ge·ne·ous mix·ture	**definition:** a substance in which components don't blend together **context:** Orange juice with pulp is one example of a **heterogeneous mixture**.
homogeneous mixture hō-mə-**jē**-nē-əs **miks**-chər ho·mo·ge·ne·ous mix·ture	**definition:** a substance in which two or more components are evenly mixed but not bonded together **context:** Air is an example of a **homogeneous mixture**.

Section 2.2: Chemistry Word List (cont.)

indicator in-di-kā-tər in·di·ca·tor	**definition:** a compound that changes color when an acid or base is present in solutions **context: Indicators** are used to determine a solution's pH.
isomer ī-sə-mər i·so·mer	**definition:** compounds with the same chemical formula but different structural formulas **context:** Many **isomers** share similar if not identical properties.
pH pē-āch p·H	**definition:** a measure of how acidic or basic a solution is; the scale ranges from 0 to 14 **context:** Vinegar is an acid and measures 4 on the **pH** scale.
product **prod**-əkt prod·uct	**definition:** the substances that result from a chemical reaction **context:** When iron, oxygen, and water chemically react, rust is the **product**.
rate of reaction rāt uv rē-ak-shən rate of re·ac·tion	**definition:** a measure of how fast a chemical reaction occurs **context:** Food spoiling is a chemical reaction, but putting food in the refrigerator slows the **rate of reaction**.
reactant rē-**ak**-tənt re·ac·tant	**definition:** a substance that undergoes a change in a chemical reaction **context:** Iron, oxygen, and water are the **reactants** when metal rusts.
saturated **sach**-ə-rāt-id sat·u·rat·ed	**definition:** a solution in which the maximum amount of solute has been dissolved **context:** Dissolving sugar in water, you reach a point where you cannot dissolve any more sugar because it becomes **saturated**.
solubility sol-yə-**bil**-i-tē sol·u·bil·i·ty	**definition:** the ability of a substance to dissolve in another substance **context:** The **solubility** of some substances can be increased by shaking or increasing temperature.
solute sol-yo͞ot sol·ute	**definition:** a substance that dissolves in a solvent **context:** In a saltwater mixture, salt is the **solute** and water is the solvent.
solution sə-**lo͞o**-shən so·lu·tion	**definition:** an evenly mixed mixture containing a solvent and at least one solute with the same properties **context:** A **solution** is also known as a homogeneous mixture.
solvent **sol**-vənt sol·vent	**definition:** a substance that dissolves the solute **context:** Water is often called the universal **solvent**.
substance **sub**-stəns sub·stance	**definition:** a single kind of matter with a fixed composition and a specific set of properties **context:** A chemical reaction produces a new **substance**.
suspension sə-**spen**-shən sus·pen·sion	**definition:** a mixture in which the components are dispersed but large enough to see and to settle out **context:** Hot chocolate is a mixture that is a **suspension**.

Section 2.2: Vocabulary Building Activities

Chemical Formulas: Scientists describe compounds using chemical formulas. The table below lists some common compounds. Copy the table in your science journal. Complete the table by writing the formula for each compound.

Compound	Formula
1. oxygen	
2. carbon dioxide	
3. sodium chloride	
4. calcium carbonate	
5. potassium nitrate	

Mixtures: A mixture is a substance made by combining two or more different substances without a chemical reaction occurring. Mixtures can be categorized as heterogeneous or homogeneous. Decide whether the mixtures listed below are heterogeneous or homogeneous. Record the answers in your science journal.

1. toothpaste   4. salad
2. perfume   5. drink mix drink
3. granite   6. Italian dressing

Chemical Bonds: When atoms form ionic or covalent compounds, they bond using electrons in their outer energy levels. Research these compounds to find out what types of bonds hold them together. Copy and complete the data table in your science journal.

Compound	Type of Bond	Definition
1. water		
2. table salt		

Types of Mixtures: Solutions, colloids, and suspensions are all mixtures. Copy and complete the data table below in your science journal.

Type of Mixture	Definition	Example
1. solution		
2. colloids		
3. suspension		

Solutions: Solutions can be made up of different combinations of solids, liquids, and gases. Copy and complete the data table below in your science journal.

Solution	State of Solvent	State of Solute	State of Solution
air			
ocean water			
cola drink			

Online Resource: "The pH Factor." Miami Museum of Science. <http://www.miamisci.org/ph/index.html>

Chemical Reactions: Chemical reactions can either release or absorb energy. An exothermic reaction releases heat and causes the temperature of the immediate surroundings to rise. An endothermic reaction absorbs heat and cools the surroundings. Copy and complete the data table below in your science journal.

Example	Type of Reaction
1. melting ice cubes	
2. rusting steel	
3. photosynthesis	
4. cooking an egg	
5. heating with coal	
6.	endothermic
7.	exothermic

Section 2.3: Force and Motion Word List

acceleration ak-sel-ə-**rā**-shən ac·cel·er·a·tion	**definition:** the change in an object's speed or direction over time **context:** The excitement of riding a roller coaster is due to unexpected **acceleration**.
Archimedes' principle är-kə-**mē**-dēz **prin**-sə-pəl Ar·chi·me·des prin·ci·ple	**definition:** a rule stating that the buoyant force on an object is equal to the weight of the fluid displaced by the object **context: Archimedes' principle** was discovered by the early Greek thinker, Archimedes, and explains why objects float.
atmospheric pressure at-mə-**sfer**-ik **presh**-ər at·mo·spher·ic pres·sure	**definition:** the weight of air caused by the force of gravity **context: Atmospheric pressure** changes with altitude.
Bernoulli's principle bər-**nōō**-lēz **prin**-sə-pəl Ber·noul·lis prin·ci·ple	**definition:** a rule stating that as the speed of a moving fluid increases, the pressure exerted by the fluid decreases **context:** Understanding **Bernoulli's principle** helped the Wright brothers design and build their plane.
buoyancy **boi**-ən-sē buoy·an·cy	**definition:** the tendency of certain objects to float **context:** A life jacket provides **buoyancy** for a swimmer.
compound machine **kom**-pound mə-**shēn** com·pound ma·chine	**definition:** a machine made from two or more simple machines **context:** A bicycle is an example of a **compound machine**.
density **den**-si-tē den·si·ty	**definition:** the measure of the amount of matter that occupies a particular space **context:** There is a correlation between what sinks and what floats in water and the **density** of the object.
fluid **flōō**-id flu·id	**definition:** a substance that has no definite shape and can flow **context:** Water is a **fluid**.
force **fôrs** force	**definition:** a push or a pull **context:** A **force** is applied to a desk to push it across the room.
free fall **frē fôl** free fall	**definition:** the movement of a falling object when the only force acting on it is gravity **context:** Regardless of mass, all objects in **free fall** accelerate at the same rate.
friction **frik**-shən fric·tion	**definition:** a force that acts to oppose sliding that occurs between two surfaces that are touching **context:** Rubbing your hands together creates **friction**.
gravity **grav**-i-tē grav·i·ty	**definition:** the force that pulls objects toward each other **context:** The force of **gravity** gives you weight.
inertia in-**ûr**-shə in·er·tia	**definition:** an object's tendency to resist a change of motion **context:** Try pushing both a hippo and a hamster, and you will find that the hippo has more **inertia**.

Section 2.3: Force and Motion Word List (cont.)

lift **lift** lift	**definition:** an upward force **context:** Large-winged planes provide more **lift** to carry heavy loads.
mass **mas** mass	**definition:** the amount of matter in an object **context:** A hippopotamus has more **mass** than a hamster.
momentum mō-**men**-təm mo·men·tum	**definition:** a measure of how hard it is to stop a moving object **context:** A baseball flying though the air has **momentum**.
motion **mō**-shən mo·tion	**definition:** an act in which one object's distance from another is changing **context:** You are in **motion** while running a race.
newton **nōōt**-n new·ton	**definition:** a unit of measure equaling the force needed to accelerate 1 kilogram of mass at 1 meter per second **context:** When you lift a small orange, you exert about one **newton** of force.
Newton's Laws of Motion **nōōt**-ns **lôz** uv **mō**-shən New·tons Laws of Mo·tion	**definition:** the rules and formulas for force, motion, acceleration, and mass **context: Newton's Laws of Motion** explain force, motion, acceleration, and mass.
Pascal's principle pas-**kals prin**-sə-pəl Pas·cals prin·ci·ple	**definition:** a principle stating that when a force is applied to an enclosed fluid, an increase in pressure is transmitted equally to all parts of the fluid **context:** One example of **Pascal's principle** is a hydraulic lift for automobiles.
power **pou**-ər pow·er	**definition:** the rate at which work is performed **context:** The unit of **power** is the watt (W).
simple machine **sim**-pəl mə-**shēn** sim·ple ma·chine	**definition:** machines that conserve the amount of work done **context:** Inclined plane, wedge, screw, lever, wheel and axle, and pulley are the six kinds of **simple machines**.
speed **spēd** speed	**definition:** the distance traveled divided by the time it takes to travel that distance **context:** A wave moving through water moves at a different **speed** than a wave moving through air.
velocity və-**los**-i-tē ve·loc·i·ty	**definition:** the speed and direction of a moving object **context:** The **velocity** of the car changes as it comes to a stop at the traffic light.
weight **wāt** weight	**definition:** the measure of the force of gravity on an object **context:** When you sit an object on a scale, it shows the pull of gravity on the object as the **weight**.
work **wûrk** work	**definition:** a force applied to an object, and the object moves as a result of the force **context:** Riding a bicycle to school is an example of **work**.

Section 2.3: Vocabulary Building Activities

Simple Machines: A lever is a common simple machine. A lever includes a fulcrum or pivot point, load or resistance (the object being moved), and force (any push or pull on an object). There are three classes of levers.

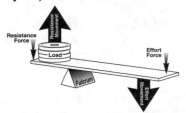
First-Class Lever

Second-Class Lever

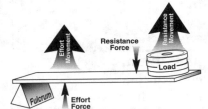
Third-Class Lever

Identify the machines below as first-class, second-class, or third-class levers. Record the answers in your science journal.

1.

2.

3.

4.

5.

6.

Newton: Motion is the act or process of moving from one place to another. Isaac Newton is the English scientist who stated the three Laws of Motion in 1687. Copy and complete the data table in your science journal.

Law	Definition	Example
First Law of Motion		
Second Law of Motion		
Third Law of Motion		

Motion: Speed is the distance traveled by a moving object in a given time. To determine speed, the distance traveled is divided by time.

Equation: $\text{Speed} = \dfrac{\text{Distance}}{\text{Time}}$

1. Find the speed of a long-distance runner who runs 30 miles in 6 hours.

_____

2. Find the speed of a train that travels a distance of 1,200 kilometers in 20 hours.

_____

Section 2.4: Energy Word List

chemical energy **kem**-i-kəl **en**-ər-jē chem·i·cal en·er·gy	**definition:** the energy stored in chemical bonds between atoms **context:** The food you eat has stored **chemical energy**.
combustion kəm-**bus**-chən com·bus·tion	**definition:** the process of burning **context:** A fuel's chemical energy is transformed into thermal energy during **combustion**.
conduction kən-**duk**-shən con·duc·tion	**definition:** the direct transfer of thermal energy between objects that touch **context:** When you stir a bowl of hot soup with a metal spoon, the spoon heats up; this is an example of **conduction**.
conserving energy kən-**sûrv**-ing **en**-ər-jē con·serv·ing en·er·gy	**definition:** the reduction of energy use **context: Conserving energy** saves money and resources.
convection kən-**vek**-shən con·vec·tion	**definition:** the transfer of thermal energy by the movement of currents within a fluid or gas **context:** When water boils in a pot, thermal energy is transferred throughout the water by **convection** currents.
electrical energy i-**lek**-tri-kəl **en**-ər-jē e·lec·tri·cal en·er·gy	**definition:** the energy carried by electric current **context:** A blender uses **electrical energy** provided by the current flowing through it.
energy **en**-ər-jē en·er·gy	**definition:** the ability to cause change **context:** You use **energy** when you dribble a ball down a basketball court.
fossil fuel **fos**-əl **fyoo**-əl fos·sil fu·el	**definition:** a fuel formed from the remains of ancient plants and animals that can be burned to produce energy **context:** Coal, formed from the remains of ancient plants, is a **fossil fuel**.
generator **jen**-ə-rā-tər gen·er·a·tor	**definition:** a device that changes mechanical energy into electrical power **context:** Enormous **generators** are located near dams.
geothermal energy jē-ō-**thûr**-məl **en**-ər-jē ge·o·ther·mal en·er·gy	**definition:** a form of heat energy generated inside Earth **context:** Many people heat their homes with **geothermal energy**.
heat **hēt** heat	**definition:** the transfer of thermal energy from one object to another **context: Heat** causes temperature to rise.
heat transfer **hēt** trans-**fûr** heat trans·fer	**definition:** the process where thermal energy moves from warmer to cooler objects **context:** Conduction, radiation, and convection are the three ways that **heat transfer** occurs.
hydroelectric energy hī-drō-i-**lek**-trik **en**-ər-jē hy·dro·e·lec·tric en·er·gy	**definition:** the potential energy of water transformed into electrical energy **context: Hydroelectric energy** is generated by dams.

Section 2.4: Energy Word List (cont.)

kinetic energy ki-**net**-ik **en**-ər-jē ki·net·ic en·er·gy	**definition:** the energy of motion **context:** The amount of **kinetic energy** an object has depends on its mass and speed.
light energy līt **en**-ər-jē light en·er·gy	**definition:** the energy carried by light and other kinds of electromagnetic waves **context: Light energy** can be absorbed, reflected, or transmitted.
nonrenewable resource non-ri-**noo**-ə-bəl rē-sōrs non·re·new·a·ble re·source	**definition:** an energy resource that is used up much faster than it can be replaced **context:** Coal, like most fossil fuels, is a **nonrenewable resource**.
nuclear energy **noo**-klē-ər **en**-ər-jē nu·cle·ar en·er·gy	**definition:** the energy contained in the nucleus of an atom **context:** During a nuclear reaction, **nuclear energy** is released.
photovoltaic fō-tō-vol-**tā**-ik pho·to·vol·ta·ic	**definition:** a device that transforms radiant energy directly into electrical energy **context:** Solar energy can be collected by **photovoltaic** cells.
potential energy pə-**ten**-shəl **en**-ər-jē po·ten·tial en·er·gy	**definition:** the stored energy in an object due to its position **context: Potential energy** is energy at rest.
radiant energy **rā**-dē-ənt **en**-ər-jē ra·di·ant en·er·gy	**definition:** the energy carried by an electromagnetic wave **context:** The sun is a source of **radiant energy**.
renewable resource ri-**noo**-ə-bil rē-sōrs re·new·a·ble re·source	**definition:** an energy resource that is replenished continually **context:** Water used to produce hydroelectricity is a **renewable resource**.
solar energy sō-lər **en**-ər-jē so·lar en·er·gy	**definition:** an inexhaustible energy source from the sun **context:** The sun is an inexhaustible source of **solar energy**.
temperature **tem**-pər-ə-chər tem·per·a·ture	**definition:** the measure of the average kinetic energy of the individual particles of a substance; the heat of a substance **context:** A thermometer is used to measure **temperature**.
thermal energy **thûr**-məl **en**-ər-jē ther·mal en·er·gy	**definition:** the sum of the kinetic and potential energy of the particles in a material **context:** The warmer a substance is, the more **thermal energy** it has.
tidal energy **tīd**-l **en**-ər-jē tid·al en·er·gy	**definition:** a nonpolluting, inexhaustible source of energy from the rise and fall of the tides in the ocean **context: Tidal energy** can only be generated in a few places.
wave wāv wave	**definition:** a disturbance that carries energy from point to point with a rhythm **context:** A sound **wave** made by a clap of thunder carries a large amount of energy.
wind wind wind	**definition:** an inexhaustible energy source from the natural movement of air **context:** Windmills are used to convert **wind** to electrical energy.

Section 2.4: Vocabulary Building Activities

Forms of Energy: Energy is a property of matter. There are many different forms of energy. Copy and complete the table below in your science journal.

Form of energy	Definition	Example
1. mechanical energy		
2. thermal energy		
3. light energy		
4. electrical energy		
5. chemical energy		
6. nuclear energy		

Resources: The earth provides many natural resources for people to use. Resources can be categorized as renewable or nonrenewable. Copy and complete the data table below in your science journal.

Resource	Renewable or Nonrenewable
1. coal	
2. wind	
3. water	
4. wood	
5. petroleum	
6. natural gas	

Heat Transfer: The three methods of heat transfer are conduction, convection, and radiation. Copy and complete the data table below in your science journal.

Example	Method of Transfer
1. sun heating the earth	
2. spoon becomes warm in a cup of hot soup	
3. heating a pot of water on the stove	

Online Resource: Discover ways to save energy at this interactive website. "Kids Saving Energy." U.S. Department of Energy. <http://www.eere.energy.gov/kids/>

Solar Energy: Clean, inexhaustible solar energy is used to cook food in countries such as Africa where other energy sources are not available. Construct a solar cooker to make s'mores using the following directions. Collect a recycled pizza or shoe box, aluminum foil, plastic wrap, glue, black spray paint, and black construction paper. Spray paint the outside of the box black. When the paint is dry, draw an 8-inch x 11-inch square on the lid of the pizza box. Cut out three sides of the square, and fold the flap back along the uncut edge to make a window in the cooker. Glue aluminum foil to the inside of this flap. Cover the window with a piece of plastic wrap. Tape the wrap to the box lid. Glue black construction paper to the inside bottom of the box. Glue foil to the inside walls of the box. Place a graham cracker in the box; stack 2 chocolate squares and a marshmallow on top of the cracker. Place the cooker in the sun. Prop the box at an angle facing the sun. Use a ruler to prop the flap open. When the chocolate has melted (10 to 15 minutes), remove the s'more, place a cracker on top of the marshmallow, and enjoy.

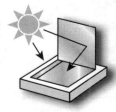

Section 2.5: Waves, Sound, and Light Word List

amplitude **am**-pli-tōōd am·pli·tude	**definition:** the maximum height of a wave crest or depth of a trough **context:** The larger the **amplitude**, the more energy carried by the wave.
color **kul**-ər col·or	**definition:** the property of reflecting light of a particular wavelength **context:** The primary **colors** are red, green, and blue.
compressed wave kəm-**prest wāv** com·pressed wave	**definition:** a type of mechanical wave in which matter in the medium moves forward and backward along the direction the wave travels **context:** Sound waves are **compressed waves**.
crest **krest** crest	**definition:** the high point of a wave **context:** Troughs are the low points of a wave and **crests** are the high points.
decibel **des**-ə-bel dec·i·bel	**definition:** a unit that measures the loudness of different sounds **context:** Listening to sounds louder than 100 **decibels** over a period of time can damage your ears.
diffraction di-**frak**-shən dif·frac·tion	**definition:** the bending and spreading of waves around a barrier **context:** Hearing a stereo playing at your neighbor's house is one example of **diffraction**.
Doppler effect **dop**-lər i-**fekt** Dop·pler ef·fect	**definition:** a change in the frequency of a sound wave that occurs when the sound source and the listener are in motion relative to each other **context:** The **Doppler effect** is used in radar guns to measure the speed of cars.
electromagnetic spectrum i-lek-trō-**mag**-net-ik **spek**-trəm e·lec·tro·mag·net·ic spec·trum	**definition:** the range of electromagnetic waves, including radio waves, visible light, and X-rays, with different frequencies and wavelengths **context:** The only part of the **electromagnetic spectrum** people can see is visible light.
electromagnetic wave i-lek-trō-**mag**-net-ik **wāv** e·lec·tro·mag·net·ic wave	**definition:** a wave of vibrating electric and magnetic fields **context:** TV and radio transmissions are examples of **electromagnetic waves**.
frequency **frē**-kwən-sē fre·quen·cy	**definition:** the number of wavelengths that pass a given point in a certain time **context: Frequency** is measured in hertz.
hertz **hûrts** hertz	**definition:** the unit in which frequency is measured **context:** A frequency of 30 **hertz** (Hz) means 30 vibrations per second.

Section 2.5: Waves, Sound, and Light Word List (cont.)

interference in-tər-**fîr**-əns in·ter·fer·ence	**definition:** the phenomenon that occurs when two waves meet while traveling along the same medium **context:** Wave interaction is called **interference**.
lens **lenz** lens	**definition:** a transparent object that has at least one curved surface that causes light to bend **context:** The more curved the sides of a **lens**, the more the light will be bent after it enters the lens.
loudness **loud**-nes loud·ness	**definition:** the human perception of how much energy a sound wave carries **context:** A volume knob controls the **loudness** of a radio.
mechanical wave mi-**kan**-i-kəl **wāv** me·chan·i·cal wave	**definition:** a type of wave that can travel only through matter **context:** Sound is a **mechanical wave** and can travel through air, solids, liquids, and gases, but not through the vacuum of outer space.
pitch **pich** pitch	**definition:** highness or lowness of sound, determined by the frequency of the wave **context:** If the **pitch** is high, the frequency is also high.
prism **priz**-əm pris·m	**definition:** a transparent device with two plane faces that are not parallel that is used to separate light **context:** A **prism** can separate white light from the sun into colors of the visible spectrum.
reflection ri-**flek**-shən re·flec·tion	**definition:** the light energy bouncing off an object or surface **context:** You can see yourself in a mirror because of the **reflection** of the light from the smooth surface of the mirror.
refraction ri-**frak**-shən re·frac·tion	**definition:** the light energy bending as it moves from one medium into another medium **context:** **Refraction** explains why stars appear to twinkle.
sound **sound** sound	**definition:** the energy transferred by an object vibrating in the air **context:** **Sound** waves create vibrations that travel through the air to your ears.
transverse wave **trans**-vûrs **wāv** trans·verse wave	**definition:** a type of mechanical wave in which the wave energy causes matter in the medium to move up and down or back and forth at right angles to the direction the wave travels **context:** An example of a **transverse wave** is a seismic wave (a type of wave that occurs during an earthquake).
trough **trof** trough	**definition:** the low point on a wave **context:** Crests are the high points of a wave, and **troughs** are the low points.
vibration vī-**brā**-shən vi·bra·tion	**definition:** the repetition of back and forth or up and down motion **context:** Sound waves create **vibrations**.
wavelength **wāv**-length wave·length	**definition:** the distance between the top of one crest to the top of the next crest (or from trough to trough) **context:** Gamma rays have the shortest **wavelength**.

Section 2.5: Vocabulary Building Activities

Light Waves: Three things can happen to light when it hits the surface of an object: bounce off, pass through, or be absorbed by the object. Identify each example in the data table as reflection, transmission, or absorption of light. Copy and complete the table in your science journal.

Example	Type of Light	Definition
1. You see a black cat.		
2. You see light shining through a window.		
3. You see yourself in a mirror.		

Waves: The highest point of a wave is called the **crest**. The lowest point is called the **trough**. The **height** of a wave is the distance from its crest to its trough. The length of a wave (**wavelength**) is the distance from its crest to the crest of the next wave. The maximum height of a wave crest or depth of a trough from the baseline is the wave's **amplitude**. Identify the parts of the wave below. Record the answers in your science journal.

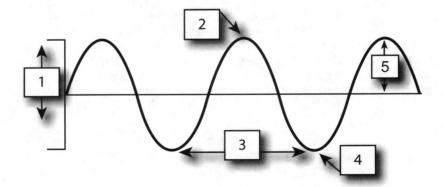

Electromagnetic Spectrum: Light travels in the form of electromagnetic waves. These waves are classified by their wavelengths. Look at the diagram at right. What is the name of the shortest wavelength? Longest? Record the answers in your science journal.

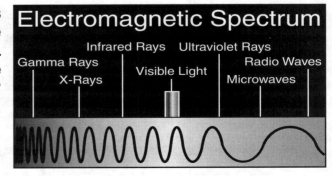

Online Resource: This interactive website illustrates the meaning of decibel levels. "Interactive Sound Ruler." National Institute on Deafness and Other Communication Disorders. <http://www. nidcd.nih.gov/health/education/decibel/decibel.asp>

Section 2.6: Electricity and Magnetism Word List

battery bat-ə-rē bat·te·ry	**definition:** a device that stores chemical energy and makes it available in an electrical form **context:** A flashlight **battery** is a single cell that carries electric current.
circuit sûr-kət cir·cuit	**definition:** a continuous path of flowing electrons from a source, through wires, and back to the source **context:** A **circuit** must be closed for current to pass through.
conductor kən-**duk**-tər con·duc·tor	**definition:** a material that allows electrons to move or that transfers heat easily **context:** Copper is a good **conductor** of electricity.
electric charge i-**lek**-trik **chärj** e·lec·tric charge	**definition:** the loss or gain of electrons from an atom **context:** There are two kinds of **electric charge**: positive and negative.
electric current i-**lek**-trik **kər**-ənt e·lec·tric cur·rent	**definition:** the rate of flow of electric charge past a given point in an electric circuit **context:** There are two kinds of **electric current**: direct current and alternating current.
electric field i-**lek**-trik **fēld** e·lec·tric field	**definiton:** the region around every electric charge that puts forth forces on other charged objects **context:** The closer you are to a charge, the stronger the **electric field.**
electric force i-**lek**-trik **fôrs** e·lec·tric force	**definition:** an attractive or repulsive force between electrically charged objects **context:** **Electric force** gets stronger between two electric charges as they get closer together.
electricity i-**lek**-**tris**-ə-tē e·lec·tric·i·ty	**definition:** the interaction between electric charges **context:** Benjamin Franklin experimented with **electricity** in the 1700s.
electric motor i-**lek**-trik **mō**-tər e·lec·tric mo·tor	**definition:** a device that transforms electrical energy into kinetic energy **context:** **Electric motors** are everywhere in your house: can opener, mixer, refrigerator.
electromagnet i-lek-trō-**mag**-nit e·lec·tro·mag·net	**definition:** a magnet made by wrapping a current-carrying wire around an iron core **context:** An **electromagnet** is responsible for making an electric doorbell ring.
generator **jen**-ə-rāt-ər gen·er·a·tor	**definition:** a device that changes mechanical energy into electrical power **context:** Enormous **generators** produce most of the electrical energy used in your home.
insulator in-sə-lā-tər in·su·la·tor	**definition:** a material that does not conduct electricity **context:** Rubber, glass, plastic, and wood are examples of **insulators** that do not conduct electricity.

Section 2.6: Electricity and Magnetism Word List (cont.)

magnet **mag**-nit mag·net	**definition:** a device used to attract or repel other objects made of iron or steel **context:** A rock containing the mineral magnetite acts as a **magnet**.
magnetic domain mag-**net**-ik dō-**mān** mag·net·ic do·main	**definition:** the magnetized region of a magnetic surface **context:** A large number of **magnetic domains** are contained in a magnet, and they are lined up and pointing in the same direction.
magnetic field mag-**net**-ik fēld mag·net·ic field	**definition:** an area that surrounds a magnet where a magnetic force can be detected **context:** All magnets are surrounded by a **magnetic field**.
magnetic force mag-**net**-ik fôrs mag·net·ic force	**definition:** an attractive or repulsive force between magnets **context:** The north pole of one magnet exerts an attractive **magnetic force** on the south pole of another magnet.
magnetism **mag**-ni-tiz-əm mag·ne·tis·m	**definition:** the property of attracting metals, producing a magnetic field by a magnet, or a conductor carrying an electric current **context: Magnetism** runs the Japanese maglev train.
magnetosphere mag-**nēt**-ə-sfîr mag·ne·to·sphere	**definition:** a region of space affected by Earth's magnetic field **context:** The **magnetosphere** deflects most charged particles from the sun.
ohms ōmz ohms	**definition:** a unit of electrical resistance **context: Ohms** are used to measure how difficult it is for electrons to flow through a material.
parallel circuit **par**-ə-lel **sûr**-kit par·al·lel cir·cuit	**definition:** a circuit that has more than one path for electric current **context:** Homes and businesses are wired using **parallel circuits**.
resistance ri-**zis**-təns re·sis·tance	**definition:** a measure of the opposition to the flow of electricity **context:** Most insulators have a much higher **resistance** than conductors.
series circuit **sîr**-ēz **sûr**-kit se·ries cir·cuit	**definition:** a circuit that has a single path for electric current **context:** Christmas lights used to be wired as a **series circuit**; when one bulb went out, all of the lights would go off.
static electricity **stat**-ik i-lek-**tris**-ə-tē stat·ic e·lec·tric·i·ty	**definition:** a buildup of charges on an object **context:** Lightning is a discharge of **static electricity**.
transformer trans-**fôr**-mər trans·for·mer	**definition:** a device used to increase or decrease voltage **context:** Most **transformers** have two coils of wire wrapped around an iron core.
voltage **vōl**-tij volt·age	**definition:** the difference in electrical potential energy between two places in a circuit; measured in volts **context: Voltage** is the amount of force pushing an electric circuit.

Section 2.6: Vocabulary Building Activities

Venn Diagram: Compare and contrast series circuits and parallel circuits. Copy and complete the Venn diagram in your science journal.

Series Circuit   Parallel Circuit

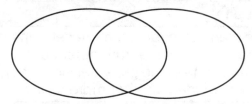

Electromagnet: Current electricity can be used to make an electromagnet. List the three ways to increase the strength of an electromagnet in your science journal.

Vocabulary Bingo: With a partner, practice the vocabulary from the Electricity and Magnetism word list.

Fold a sheet of white paper into 4 vertical columns. Unfold the paper. Now fold the paper into 4 horizontal rows. Unfold the paper.

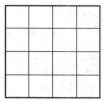

Write "Free" in one of the squares. Fill in the remaining squares with vocabulary words. The caller reads a definition. The player searches for the matching vocabulary word on the bingo sheet. When the player finds a match, a bean is placed on the square. When the player has filled in the squares in a diagonal, vertical or horizontal pattern on the card, the player yells, "Bingo!"

Circuits: An electrical circuit is a complete path through which electrons flow from an energy source. Two kinds of basic circuits are series and parallel. Identify each type of circuit shown below and write the answer in your science journal. Answer the questions that follow in your science journal, as well.

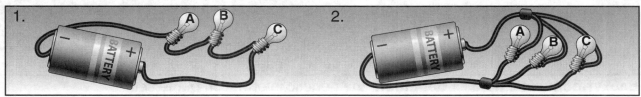

3. What will happen if bulb B is removed from circuit number 1?
4. What will happen if bulb C is removed from circuit number 2?

Ohms: George Ohm, a physicist, discovered a very important relationship between voltage (V), current (I), and resistance (R). Voltage is measured in volts, current is measured in amps, and resistance is measured in ohms. Electricians use Ohm's Law to determine the efficiency of electrical circuits for safety purposes.

Equation: $V = I \times R$

Calculate:

If you have a current of 1.2 amps flowing through a device with a resistance of 10 ohms, the voltage is _____.

Section 3.1: Structure of Life Word List

cell metabolism sel mə-**tab**-ə-liz-əm cell me·tab·o·lis·m	**definition:** the activities carried out by a cell **context: Cell metabolism** includes releasing energy from food, making chemicals the cell needs, and getting rid of wastes.
cellular respiration **sel**-yə-lər res-pə-**rā**-shən cel·lu·lar res·pi·ra·tion	**definition:** the process in which oxygen is chemically combined with food molecules in the cell to release energy **context:** Both plant and animal cells get energy in the form they need through **cellular respiration.**
Cell Theory sel **thîr**-ē Cell Theor·y	**definition:** an organism is made up of one or more cells, the cell is the basic unit of life, and all cells come from other cells **context: Cell Theory** provides one of the great unifying theories in biology—all organisms are made of one or more cells.
cell wall sel wôl cell wall	**definition:** a structure that surrounds the cell membrane in plants; provides shape and support **context:** The **cell wall** is a stiff protective layer around the cell membrane of plant cells.
chlorophyll **klôr**-ə-fil chlor·o·phyll	**definition:** a green chemical in the leaf that allows plants to trap the sun's energy **context: Chlorophyll** is the green chemical in plant cells that help them make their own food.
chloroplast **klôr**-ə-plast chlor·o·plast	**definition:** a disc-shaped organelle in plant cells; gives plants green color and contains chlorophyll, helping plants make food **context: Chloroplasts** are the food-making structures of the plant cell.
chromosome **krō**-mə-sōm chro·mo·some	**definition:** the structure in the nucleus that contains the genetic information that directs cell activity **context:** Humans have 23 pairs of **chromosomes.**
cytoplasm **sī**-tə-plaz-əm cy·to·plas·m	**definition:** a gel-like material that contains proteins, nutrients, and all of the other cell organelles **context:** The **cytoplasm** is where the food, water, and oxygen taken in by the cell are used.
deoxyribonucleic acid dē-ok-sē-**rī**-bō-nōō-klē-ik **as**-id de·ox·y·ri·bo·nu·cle·ic ac·id	**definition:** the genetic information of the cell **context:** The traits that make organisms different from one another are contained in the DNA (**deoxyribonucleic acid**).
diffusion dif-**yōō**-zhən dif·fu·sion	**definition:** the movement of molecules into and out of the cell **context:** The process of **diffusion** helps the cell carry out all the basic life activities.
endoplasmic reticulum en-də-**plaz**-mik ri-**tik**-yə-ləm en·do·plas·mic re·tic·u·lum	**definition:** the transportation system for the cell **context:** The **endoplasmic reticulum** transports materials within the cell.
eukaryotic cell yōō-kar-ē-**ot**-ik sel eu·kar·y·ot·ic cell	**definition:** a single cell with a nucleus **context:** All organisms, except bacteria, are made up of **eukaryotic cells.**

Section 3.1: Structure of Life Word List (cont.)

Golgi body gôl-jē bod-ē Gol·gi bod·y	**definition:** a structure that packages and distributes protein outside the cell **context:** The **Golgi body** packages proteins for the cell.
mitochondria mī-tə-**kon**-drē-ə mi·to·chon·dri·a	**definition:** organelles that provide the cell with energy **context:** The **mitochondria** are called the "power houses" of the cell because they provide the cell with energy.
molecule **mol**-i-kyo͞ol mol·e·cule	**definition:** the smallest particle of a substance **context:** **Molecules** can go in and out of the cell by moving through the tiny holes in the cell membrane.
multicellular mul-ti-**sel**-yə-lər mul·ti·cel·lu·lar	**definition:** an organism made up of many cells **context:** Snails, fish, trees, and humans are all **multicellular** organisms.
nuclear membrane no͞o-klē-ər mem-brān nu·cle·ar mem·brane	**definition:** the membrane that surrounds the nucleus **context:** The **nuclear membrane** is often referred to as the nuclear envelope because it envelops the nucleus.
nucleolus no͞o-**klē**-ə-ləs nu·cle·o·lus	**definition:** the structure in the nucleus responsible for making ribosomes **context:** The ribosomes are produced in the **nucleolus** of the cell.
nucleus no͞o-klē-əs nu·cle·us	**definition:** the control center for the cell **context:** The **nucleus** is usually located near the center of the cell and controls the activity of the cell.
organelle ôr-gə-**nel** or·ga·nelle	**definition:** any of the tiny structures in the cytoplasm, each does a specific job for the cell **context:** **Organelles** are scattered throughout the cell's cytoplasm.
osmosis oz-**mō**-sis os·mo·sis	**definition:** the movement of water molecules into and out of cells **context:** **Osmosis** is the process that allows water molecules to move into and out of a cell.
plasma membrane **plaz**-mə **mem**-brān plas·ma mem·brane	**definition:** a thin layer that encloses the cell and controls what enters and leaves the cell **context:** Tiny pores in the **plasma membrane** allow food, water, and oxygen to pass into the cell and waste to pass out.
prokaryotic cell prō-kar-ē-**ot**-ik **sel** pro·kar·y·ot·ic cell	**definition:** a cell that has no nucleus; the DNA and other materials are scattered throughout the cytoplasm **context:** Bacteria are a good example of **prokaryotic cells**.
ribosome **rī**-bə-sōm ri·bo·some	**definition:** an organelle that makes protein for the cell **context:** A **ribosome** makes proteins that will be used inside the cell.
unicellular yo͞o-ni-**sel**-yə-lər u·ni·cel·lu·lar	**definition:** an organism made up of only one cell **context:** Many organisms, including bacteria, are **unicellular**.
vacuole vak-yo͞o-ōl vac·u·ole	**definition:** a structure that stores food, water, and waste for the cell **context:** Plant cells usually have only one large **vacuole**.

Section 3.1: Vocabulary Building Activities

Plant and Animal Cells: Identify the organelles of the plant and animal cell below. Some organelles will be used more than once. Record the answers in your science journal.

4. control center for the cell

10. surrounds the cell membrane; provides shape and support for the cell

1. packages and distributes protein outside the cell

5. thin layer that encloses the cell and controls what enters and leaves the cell

12. network of tubes that makes up the transportation system for the cell

6. stores food, water, and waste for the cell

7. gel-like material that contains proteins, nutrients, and all the other organelles

2. makes protein for the cell

Animal Cell

8. makes energy for the cell

Plant Cell

13. makes protein for the cell

3. network of tubes that makes up the transportation system for the cell

9. packages and distributes protein outside the cell

11. contains chlorophyll that helps plants make food; gives plants green color

3-D Plant and Animal Cells: Line two clean school milk cartons with sandwich bags. Allow the excess part of the bag to extend over the edges of the milk cartons. Mix lemon gelatin according to the directions on the package. Pour half of the cooled gelatin into each lined carton. When the mixture begins to gel, gently push a variety of candies (marshmallows, gummy worms, jelly beans, rope licorice, and other candies) into the gelatin to represent the organelles of a plant and animal cell. Once the mixture has completely cooled, close the sandwich bags. Let the gelatin set overnight in a refrigerator. The next day, take the cell that represents an animal cell out of the milk carton. Leave the plant cell in the carton. (The milk carton will represent the cell wall for your plant cell.) Create a key for each cell.

Online Resource: Learn more about cells, take a virtual tour of a cell, and hear the correct pronunciations of difficult cell terms at the site below.
"The Virtual Cell; Cell Biology." University of North Carolina.
<http://www.ibiblio.org/virtualcell/tour/ cell/cell.htm>

Section 3.1: Vocabulary Building Activities (cont.)

Venn Diagram: Compare and contrast the structure of a plant and animal cell. Copy and complete the Venn diagram in your science journal.

Plant and Animal Cell Venn Diagram

Why do plant cells have a cell wall and animal cells do not? Answer in your science journal.

Diffusion: Select four balloons and liquid food flavoring: vanilla, maple, banana, and coconut. Using a funnel, add a couple of drops of one flavoring to a balloon. Blow up the balloon and tie the end. Complete the procedure for each of the other food flavorings. After several minutes, smell the balloons. Answer the questions below in your science journal.

1. How did the smell of the food flavorings escape the balloons?
2. Compare the activity to diffusion that occurs in cells.

Plant and Animal Cell: Observe the structure of a plant and animal cell.

Plant Cell

Peel the thin clear tissue from the inside section of an onion. Carefully place the tissue flat on a slide. Gently smooth out any wrinkles in the tissue. Add a drop of iodine to the tissue. View the tissue under the microscope.

Animal Cell

Add a drop of iodine to a slide. Use the blunt end of a toothpick to gently scrape the inside lining of your cheek. Place the blunt end of the toothpick on the slide and mix it with the iodine. Place a cover slip over the solution. View the slide under the microscope.

Copy the table below. Record your observations about plant and animal cells in your science journal.

Cell	Drawing	Description
plant		
animal		

What similarities did you observe when viewing the plant and animal cells? Answer in your science journal.

Types of Cells: There are two main types of cells: eukaryotic and prokaryotic. Copy and complete the table below in your science journal.

Cell Type	Definition	Example
eukaryotic cell 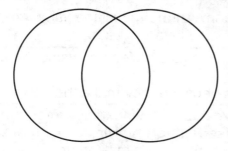		
prokaryotic cell		

Section 3.2: Classification Word List

angiosperm **an**-jē-ə-spûrm an·gi·o·sperm	**definition:** a plant that produces flowers with the seeds enclosed in the fruit **context: Angiosperms** are divided into two classes: monocots and dicots.
Animalia **an**-ə-məl-ə An·i·mal·ia	**definition:** the classification kingdom having multicellular organisms, cells that lack a cell wall, are able to move about, and possess a nervous system **context:** Members of the kingdom **Animalia** include fish, birds, mammals, reptiles, amphibians, and invertebrates.
autotroph ô-tə-trof au·to·troph	**definition:** an organism that makes its own food by using the sun's energy **context:** Trees are **autotrophs** because they make their own food.
classification hierarchy klas-ə-fi-**kā**-shən **hī**-ə-rär-kē clas·si·fi·ca·tion hi·e·rar·chy	**definition:** a system used to organize all living things into groups **context:** Scientists use the **classification hierarchy** to organize all organisms into the five kingdoms: plants, animals, fungi, protists, and monerans.
dichotomous key dī-**kot**-ə-məs **kē** di·chot·o·mous key	**definition:** a tool that helps identify unknown organisms in the natural world, such as trees, wildflowers, mammals, reptiles, rocks, and fish **context:** A **dichotomous key** has several pairs of statements that describe an organism; the user chooses the appropriate statements from each pair in order to identify an organism.
endoskeleton en-dō-**skel**-i-tən en·do·skel·e·ton	**definition:** the internal skeleton of an organism **context:** The endoskeleton of a mammal helps support the body and protect the organs.
exoskeleton ek-sō-**skel**-i-tən ex·o·skel·e·ton	**definition:** an outside skeleton found on arthropods **context:** An **exoskeleton** makes it possible for arthropods to live on land without drying out.
Fungi **fun**-jī Fun·gi	**definition:** the members of a kingdom that contain one-celled and many-celled living things that absorb food from their environment **context:** Members of the kingdom **Fungi** are responsible for the decay and decomposition of living matter.
gymnosperm **jim**-nə-spûrm gym·no·sperm	**definition:** a seed plant that does not produce flowers **context:** Redwood trees, the tallest and one of the oldest trees in the world, are **gymnosperms**.
heterotroph **het**-ə-ro-trōf het·e·ro·troph	**definition:** an organism that gets energy from eating plants and/or other animals **context:** In the food chain, a **heterotroph** is a consumer.
invertebrate in-**vûr**-tə-brāt in·ver·te·brate	**definition:** an animal that does not have a backbone **context:** An earthworm is classified as an **invertebrate** because it does not have a backbone.

Section 3.2: Classification Word List (cont.)

Monera mō-**nir**-ā Mo·ner·a	**definition:** a one-celled organism that has no nucleus **context:** All members of the kingdom **Monera** are bacteria.
nonvascular non-**vas**-kyə-lər non·vas·cu·lar	**definition:** a plant that does not have tube-like structures to carry food and water **context: Nonvascular** plants do not have stems or roots.
photosynthesis fō-tō-**sin**-thi-sis pho·to·syn·the·sis	**definition:** the food-making process in green plants that uses sunlight **context:** During **photosynthesis**, carbon dioxide, sunlight, and water combine with chlorophyll to produce glucose.
Plantae **plant**-ā Plant-ae	**definition:** the kingdom that contains complex, multicellular organisms, usually green, that use the sun's energy to make their own food **context:** A tree, which is green and makes its own food, is a member of the kingdom **Plantae**.
pollination pol-ə-nā-shən pol·li·na·tion	**definition:** the transfer of a pollen grain to the egg-producing part of a plant **context:** Some flowering plants depend on the wind for **pollination**.
Protista **prō**-tist-ə Pro·tist·a	**definition:** the kingdom that includes unicellular eukaryotic organisms that cannot be classified into any of the other eukaryotic kingdoms **context:** The **Protista** kingdom includes organisms such as protozoa, algae, euglena, and paramecium.
respiration res-pə-**rā**-shən res·pi·ra·tion	**definition:** the release of energy in plants and animals from food (sugar) **context: Respiration** allows plants and animals to use the energy stored in food.
symmetry **sim**-i-trē sym·me·try	**definition:** the balanced distribution of duplicate body parts or shapes **context:** Invertebrates have two basic body types of **symmetry**: radial **symmetry** or bilateral **symmetry**.
taxonomy tak-**son**-ə-mē tax·on·o·my	**definition:** the science of classifying organisms **context:** Charles Linnaeus, a Swedish physician and botanist, founded the science of **taxonomy**.
transpiration tran-spi-**rā**-shən tran·spi·ra·tion	**definition:** the evaporation of water from a plant **context:** During **transpiration**, water is released into the atmosphere through the stomata.
tropism **trō**-piz-əm tro·pis·m	**definition:** a response of a plant toward or away from a stimulus **context:** A plant's growth in response to gravity, light, or touch is called **tropism**.
vascular **vas**-kyə-lər vas·cu·lar	**definition:** a plant with tube-like structures inside the plant used to carry food, water, and minerals **context: Vascular** plants have leaves, stems, and roots.
vertebrate **vûr**-tə-brāt ver·te·brate	**definition:** an animal that has a backbone **context:** A lizard is classified as a **vertebrate** because it has a backbone.

Section 3.2: Vocabulary Building Activities

Leaf Food Factory: Photosynthesis (the process plants use to make food) happens in the leaf. The green leaves absorb light energy from the sun. They also take in carbon dioxide from the air through the **stomata** (openings) in the leaf. Water and minerals from the soil travel through the roots and stems of the plant to mix with chlorophyll, sunlight, and carbon dioxide to produce **glucose** (sugar). Draw a diagram explaining the process of photosynthesis in your science journal.

Angiosperms and Gymnosperms: Divide a sheet of drawing paper in half. Label one half *angiosperms* and the other half *gymnosperms.* Using magazines and seed catalogs, cut out plant pictures and glue them under the correct heading on the paper.

Vascular vs. Nonvascular: Identify plants with stems and roots and those without. Copy and complete the data table below.

Plant	Description	Example
vascular		
nonvascular		

Vertebrate vs. Invertebrate: Make a study aide to help you remember the difference between vertebrates and invertebrates. Fold a sheet of white paper in half like a hotdog bun. Fold the paper in half again, from side to side. Unfold the paper and cut up the fold making two flaps. On the front of one flap, write invertebrate and on the other, write vertebrate. Under the flaps, write the definitions and give examples of each type of animal.

Dichotomous Tree Key: Use the key at the following website to see if you can identify the trees in your neighborhood. "Dichotomous Tree Key." Wisconsin Department of Natural Resources. <http://www.dnr.state.wi.us/org/caer/ce/eek/veg/treekey/index.htm>

Venn Diagram: Compare and contrast the processes of plant respiration and transpiration. Copy and complete the Venn diagram below in your science journal.

Respiration   Transpiration

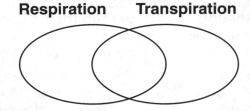

Classification Hierarchy: Create a mnemonic device to help you remember the levels of classification.

Levels	Example	Your Mnemonic
Kingdom	**K**eep	K
Phylum	**P**utting	P
Class	**C**ookies	C
Order	**O**ut	O
Family	**F**or	F
Genus	**G**irl	G
Species	**S**couts	S

Simple Organisms: Some groups of organisms: monerans, protista, and fungi, do not have complex sturctures. This makes them easy for scientists to study using a microscope. Copy and complete the data table in your science journal.

Kingdom	Characteristics	Examples
1. Monera		
2. Fungi		
3. Protista		

Section 3.3: Life Cycles Word List

ametabolous am-e-tab-o-lous am·e·tab·o·lous	**definition:** the life cycle of an insect where there is slight or no metamorphosis, only the egg stage and the adult stage **context:** Silverfish are considered **ametabolous** because they start as an egg and then hatch looking like an adult.
angiosperm **an**-jē-ə-spûrm an·gi·o·sperm	**definition:** a plant that produces flowers with the seeds enclosed in the fruit **context:** An apple tree is an **angiosperm**.
complete metamorphosis kəm-**plēt** met-ə-**môr**-fə-sis com·plete met·a·mor·pho·sis	**definition:** a life cycle including four stages: egg, larva, pupa, and adult **context:** A butterfly goes through the stages of **complete metamorphosis**.
cone **kōn** cone	**definition:** a seed-bearing structure of conifer plants **context:** Seeds can be found in the **cones** of a pine tree.
egg eg egg	**definition:** the female sex cell **context:** Female moths can lay hundreds of fertilized **eggs** on a single leaf.
embryo **em**-brē-ō em·bry·o	**definition:** an early stage of development in an organism **context:** In humans, a fertilized egg cell divides into many different cells to form an **embryo**.
fertilization fûr-tl-i-**zā**-shən fer·til·i·za·tion	**definition:** a sperm cell joining with an egg cell **context:** After **fertilization**, angiosperms produce seeds within the fruit.
flower **flou**-ər flow·er	**definition:** the part of the plant that performs the job of reproduction **context:** The **flower** is the reproductive structure found in flowering plants.
fruit **frōōt** fruit	**definition:** the plant part that carries and protects the seeds **context:** Angiosperms produce their seeds within a **fruit**.
gametophyte gə-**mē**-tə-fīt ga·me·to·phyte	**definition:** the stage in the life cycle of a plant that produces two types of sex cells—sperm cells and egg cells **context:** The **gametophytes** produce sex cells.
germination jûr-mə-**nā**-shən ger·mi·na·tion	**definition:** the time it takes for a seed to sprout **context:** Seed **germination** depends on three factors: temperature, moisture, and oxygen.
gestation je-**stā**-shən ges·ta·tion	**definition:** the process of mammals carrying their young in the womb where the fetus develops until it is born **context:** The period of **gestation** for an elephant is about 645 days.

Section 3.3: Life Cycles Word List (cont.)

gymnosperm **jim**-nə-spûrm gym·no·sperm	**definition:** a seed plant that does not produce flowers **context:** Redwood trees, the tallest and one of the oldest trees in the world, are **gymnosperms**.
incomplete metamorphosis in-kəm-**plēt** met-ə-**môr**-fə-sis in·com·plete met·a·mor·pho·sis	**definition:** a life cycle with three stages: egg, nymph, and adult **context:** Dragonflies go through the stages of **incomplete metamorphosis**.
insect **in**-sekt in·sect	**definition:** an arthropod that develops from an egg to an adult through the process of metamorphosis **context:** **Insects** change form through the process of metamorphosis.
life cycle **līf sī**-kəl life cy·cle	**definition:** the stages in an organism's life that include being born, developing into an adult, reproducing, and eventually dying **context:** The stages in the **life cycle** of a butterfly include egg, larva, pupa, and adult.
metamorphosis met-ə-**môr**-fə-sis met·a·mor·pho·sis	**definition:** the change in shape and appearance of an insect or other animal at each stage of its life cycle **context:** Egg, larva, pupa, and adult are the four stages of **metamorphosis**.
plant **plant** plant	**definition:** organism that has cell walls, makes its own food through photosynthesis, and reproduces through seeds or spores **context:** Ferns, daisies, and maple trees are all kinds of **plants**.
pollination pol-ə-**nā**-shən pol·li·na·tion	**definition:** the transfer of a pollen grain to the egg-producing part of a plant **context:** Some flowering plants depend on the wind for **pollination**.
seed **sēd** seed	**definition:** an undeveloped plant with stored food sealed in a protective covering **context:** A **seed** has three parts: seed coat, cotyledon, and embryo.
sex cell **seks sel** sex cell	**definition:** the egg and sperm cell **context:** During the life cycle of a pine tree, the **sex cells** are produced in the cones.
simple life cycle **sim**-pəl **līf sī**-kəl sim·ple life cy·cle	**definition:** a life cycle with three stages—before birth, young, and adult **context:** Most animals, including fish, mammals, reptiles, and birds, have **simple life cycles**.
spore **spôr** spore	**definition:** the cells in seedless plants that grow into new organisms **context:** The **spores** of a fern are easily spread by the wind.
sporophyte spôr-ə-**fīt** spor·o·phyte	**definition:** the spore-producing stage of reproduction for plants like ferns **context:** In fern reproduction, the fertilized egg cell grows into a **sporophyte**.

Section 3.3: Vocabulary Building Activities

Vocabulary Code Puzzle: Decode the life cycle vocabulary words using the code below. Record the answers in your science journal.

a	b	c	d	e	f	g	h	i	j	k	l	m	n	o	p	q	r	s	t	u	v	w	x	y	z
13	4	20	1	11	2	16	5	18	3	22	8	19	26	17	21	6	24	10	9	25	15	23	7	12	14

1. 11-7-17-10-22-11-8-11-9-17-26
2. 19-11-9-13-19-17-24-21-5-17-10-18-10
3. 18-26-10-11-20-9
4. 11-16-16
5. 2-8-17-23-11-24

Create your own alphabet code puzzle. Code five life cycle vocabulary words. Trade your puzzle with a partner. Try solving the new code puzzle.

Fern Life Cycle: Ferns spend one part of their life in the sporophyte stage (the sporophyte releases spores, and spores grow into gametophytes) and the other half in the gametophyte stage (gametophyte produces sex cells, sperm cells fertilize an egg, fertilized egg grows into a saprophyte). Draw and label a fern life cycle diagram in your science journal.

Venn Diagram: Copy the Venn diagram below in your science journal. Compare complete and incomplete metamorphosis for insects.

Metamorphosis

Complete   **Incomplete**

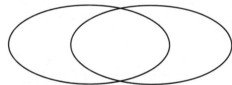

Online Resource: Learn about the life cycle of a salmon at the following website. "Interactive Salmon Life Cycle." Bonneville Power Administration. <http://www.streamnet.org/pub-ed/ff/Factsheets/Lifecycle.html>

Animal Life Cycles: Animals reproduce to make more of their own kind. The stages in the life of an animal as it grows, develops, and matures vary for different kinds of organisms. Copy and complete the data table below in your science journal. Place **simple life cycle**, **complete metamorphosis**, **incomplete metamorphosis**, or **ametabolous** in the "Life Cycle" column for each animal.

Animal	Stages	Life Cycle
1. mosquito	egg/larva/pupa/adult	
2. dragonfly	egg/larva/adult	
3. frog	egg/tadpole/adult	
4. eagle	egg/chick/adult	
5. snake	egg/snakelet/adult	
6. silverfish	egg/adult	

Section 3.3: Vocabulary Building Activities (cont.)

Frogs: Draw and describe the three stages in the life cycle of a frog.

Life Cycle Stage

	Description: _____ _____ _____ _____
	Description: _____ _____ _____ _____
	Description: _____ _____ _____ _____

Spores: Ferns reproduce from spores, not flowers. On the underside of a fertile fern frond are clusters of brown dots. The dots are made up of many spore cases. Examine a fern frond with spore cases. Use a toothpick to open a spore case. Examine the spores with a magnifying glass. Record observations in your science journal.

Pine Cones: Pine tree seeds are found inside of the cones on the upper surface of each scale. Collect several pine cones. Open pine cones have already dropped their seeds, so look for and collect cones that are still closed. Look on the ground around pine trees for ripe cones, sometime in the summer or early fall. After you collect the ripe cones,  lay them out in the sun to dry. Once dry, the cones will open. Then place them in a paper bag and shake the cones to release the seeds. Examine the seeds and record observations in your science journal.

Section 3.4: Reproduction and Heredity Word List

allele ə-**lēl** al·lele	**definition:** different variations of a gene **context: Alleles** are a combination of dominant and recessive traits for a gene.
asexual reproduction ā-**sek**-shoo-əl rē-prə-duk-shən a·sex·u·al re·pro·duc·tion	**definition:** a single parent produces offspring that are identical to the parent **context:** Budding in plants is an example of **asexual reproduction**.
cell division sel di-**vizh**-ən cell di·vis·ion	**definition:** the process in reproduction and growth by which a cell divides to form two identical cells **context: Cell division** allows an organism to grow larger.
chromatid **krō**-mə-tid chro·ma·tid	**definition:** the identical copy of a chromosome **context:** During cell division, two **chromatids** are formed when chromosomes duplicate.
chromosome **krō**-mə-sōm chro·mo·some	**definition:** the structure in the nucleus that contains the genetic information that directs cell activity **context:** Humans have 23 pairs of **chromosomes**.
cytokinesis sī-tō-ki-**nē**-sis cy·to·ki·ne·sis	**definition:** the process where cytoplasm divides, forming two identical cells **context:** During **cytokinesis**, two identical cells are formed.
daughter cell **dô**-tər sel daugh·ter cell	**definition:** the new cells formed when a cell divides **context:** During mitosis, the divided cell forms two new cells called **daughter cells**.
deoxyribonucleic acid dē-ok-sē-**rī**-bō-noo-klē-ik **as**-id de·ox·y·ri·bo·nu·cle·ic acid	**definition:** the genetic information of the cell **context:** The traits that make organisms different from one another are contained in the **deoxyribonucleic acid** (DNA).
dominant **dom**-ə-nənt dom·i·nant	**definition:** the stronger of two traits in an organism **context:** A **dominant gene** gives people brown eyes rather than blue eyes.
fertilization fûr-tl-ī-**zā**-shən fer·til·i·za·tion	**definition:** a sperm cell joins with an egg cell **context:** It is a matter of chance which sperm and egg cell will join during **fertilization**.
gamete **gam**-ēt gam·ete	**definition:** the reproductive cells: egg and sperm **context: Gametes** contain only half the normal number of chromosomes as normal cells.
gene jēn gene	**definition:** the small section of a chromosome that determines a trait **context: Genes** carry the hereditary instructions for the cell.
genetics jə-**net**-iks ge·net·ics	**definition:** the study of how traits are passed from parent to offspring **context: Genetics** explain how organisms inherit traits.
genotype **jē**-nə-tīp ge·no·type	**definition:** the inherited combination of alleles in an offspring **context:** The **genotype** for the height of a tall pea plant may be *TT* or *Tt*.

Section 3.4: Reproduction and Heredity Word List (cont.)

heredity hə-**red**-i-tē he·red·i·ty	**definition:** the passing of traits from parents to offspring **context:** The process of **heredity** occurs among all living things including animals, plants, bacteria, protists, and fungi.
inherited trait in-**her**-it-əd **trāt** in·her·it·ed trait	**definition:** a characteristic passed from parent to offspring **context:** Hair and skin color are examples of **inherited traits**.
Law of Dominance lô uv **dom**-ə-nəns Law of Dom·i·nance	**definition:** the principles of genetics **context:** The study of the inherited traits of pea plants by Gregor Mendel led to the **Law of Dominance**.
meiosis mī-**ō**-sis mei·o·sis	**definition:** the process of sex cell formation **context:** **Meiosis** only happens in reproductive cells.
Mendel, Gregor men-**dəl greg**-ər Men·del Greg·or	**definition:** a scientist who studied genetic patterns in pea plants **context:** **Gregor Mendel** is often called the "father of modern genetics" for his study of the traits of pea plants.
Mendelian trait men-**dē**-lē-ən **trāt** Men·de·li·an trait	**definition:** a trait produced by a single gene **context:** Hair color is a common **Mendelian trait**.
mitosis mī-**tō**-sis mi·to·sis	**definition:** the process of cell division: interphase, prophase, metaphase, anaphase, telophase **context:** **Mitosis** allows living things to grow and repair themselves by producing new cells.
mutation myōō-**tā**-shən mu·ta·tion	**definition:** the changes in a gene **context:** An albino alligator is an example of a gene **mutation** that changes the coloring of skin cells.
nucleus **nōō**-klē-əs nu·cle·us	**definition:** a part of the cell responsible for growth and reproduction **context:** During cell division, the **nucleus** divides.
phenotype **fē**-nə-tīp phe·no·type	**definition:** the physical appearance of an organism **context:** The **phenotype** for the height of a tall pea plant is tall, whether the plant's alleles are *TT* or *Tt*.
Punnett square pə-nət **skwâr** Pun·nett square	**definition:** a square designed to predict all possible gene combinations for the offspring of two parents **context:** Scientists use a **Punnett square** to predict all possible gene combinations for flower color in the offspring.
recessive ri-**ses**-iv re·ces·sive	**definition:** a trait that is hidden; the weaker of two traits **context:** Earlobes being directly attached to a person's head is caused by a **recessive** gene.
sexual reproduction **sek**-shōō-əl **rē**-prə-duk-shən sex·u·al re·pro·duc·tion	**definition:** a new cell formed when DNA from both parents combine **context:** **Sexual reproduction** requires two parents.
trait **trāt** trait	**definition:** a characteristic **context:** Mendel studied pea plants to determine how the **traits** of the parent plants were passed on to their offspring.

Section 3.4: Vocabulary Building Activities

Mendelian Traits: Your genes [units in the chromosomes that contain your dominant (D) and recessive (r) traits] have been inherited from your parents. Below is a fun list of some common Mendelian Traits. Do you have any of these traits? Which parent has these traits? Record the answers in your science journal.

Mendelian Trait	You	Mother	Father
Tongue Rolling (D): ability to roll tongue into a longitudinal u-shaped tube	Yes/No	Yes/No	Yes/No
Dimples (D): natural smile produces dimples in one or both cheeks or a dimple in the center of the chin	Yes/No	Yes/No	Yes/No
Attached Earlobes (r): earlobes directly attached to head	Yes/No	Yes/No	Yes/No
Freckles (D): circular pattern of skin coloration	Yes/No	Yes/No	Yes/No
Second Toe Longest (D): second toe is longer than the big toe	Yes/No	Yes/No	Yes/No

Inherited Traits vs. Acquired Traits: Some traits are inherited. Some traits are acquired throughout the course of a person's lifetime. Learned behaviors are examples of acquired traits. Decide whether the trait described is an acquired trait or an inherited trait. Copy and complete the data table in your science journal.

Trait	Acquired or Inherited
1. does not like broccoli	
2. has freckles	
3. has green eyes	
4. can hit a baseball	

DNA: Blend together 1 cup chopped onions, 30 mL warm water, and 1 teaspoon salt for 5–10 seconds. Do not totally liquefy. Pour mixture through a strainer into a clear glass beaker. Add 30 mL liquid dish soap and mix gently with a toothpick for 3–5 minutes. Do not make bubbles. Add 1/8 teaspoon meat tenderizer to the liquid. Stir gently. Add rubbing alcohol to the mixture. Slowly pour it down the side of the beaker so the alcohol forms a separate layer on top of the onion mixture. Pour until you have the same amount of alcohol in the beaker as the onion mixture. The clear, gooey strings floating to the top are DNA. The strands may have small bubbles attached to them. Slowly twist a strand onto a toothpick. (Do not scoop up scum from below the alcohol layer.) Observe the DNA under a microscope. Record observations in your science journal.

Online Resource: View an animated version of meiosis and mitosis at the following website. "Comparison of Meiosis and Mitosis." McGraw-Hill Companies, Inc.
<http://highered.mcgraw-hill.com/sites/0072437316/student_view0/chapter12/animations.html#>

Section 3.5: Ecology Word List

abiotic factor ā-bī-**ot**-ik **fak**-tər a·bi·ot·ic fac·tor	**definition:** a nonliving part of an ecosystem **context:** Water is an **abiotic factor** in an ecosystem.
adapt ə-**dapt** a·dapt	**definition:** to change because of a certain situation in the environment **context:** Dinosaurs were not able to **adapt** to changes in their environment.
adaptation ad-ap-**tā**-shən ad·ap·ta·tion	**definition:** a characteristic that enables a living thing to survive in its environment **context:** Chameleons change color; this is a protective **adaptation**.
biosphere **bī**-ə-sfîr bi·o·sphere	**definition:** the part of the earth that supports life **context:** The **biosphere** extends up into the atmosphere and deep down to the ocean floor.
biotic factor bī-**ot**-ik **fak**-tər bi·ot·ic fac·tor	**definition:** a living part of the ecosystem **context:** Animals that fill the niche of predator and prey are examples of **biotic factors** that affect an ecosystem.
camouflage **kam**-ə-fläzh cam·ou·flage	**definition:** an adaptation in which an animal protects itself against predators by blending in with the environment **context: Camouflage** helps some caterpillars look like twigs.
climax community **klī**-maks kə-**myōō**-ni-tē cli·max com·mu·ni·ty	**definition:** the final stage of succession in an area **context:** The forest was considered a **climax community** because it had reached the final stage of succession.
commensalism kə-**men**-sə-liz-əm com·men·sa·lis·m	**definition:** a relationship between two kinds of organisms that benefits one without harming the other **context:** The relationship between a Monarch butterfly and a milkweed is an example of **commensalism**.
community kə-**myōō**-ni-tē com·mu·ni·ty	**definition:** the living things in an ecosystem **context:** The various populations of living things in an ecosystem form a **community**.
diversity di-**vûr**-si-tē di·ver·si·ty	**definition:** a wide variety of traits in individuals from the same population **context:** When members of a species have differences, this is called **diversity**.
ecological succession ē-kə-**lo**-ji-kəl sək-**sesh**-ən e·co·lo·gi·cal suc·cess·ion	**definition:** the gradual replacement of one community by another **context:** The **ecological succession** of the grassland to a deciduous forest took hundreds of years.
ecology i-**kol**-ə-jē e·col·o·gy	**definition:** the study of how living and nonliving things interact **context:** The students studied the **ecology** of the river.

Section 3.5: Ecology Word List (cont.)

ecosystem ē-kō-sis-təm e·co·sys·tem	**definition:** the interaction of all the living and nonliving things in an environment **context:** The forest **ecosystem** was damaged by the fire.
energy pyramid en-ər-jē **pir**-ə-mid en·er·gy pyr·a·mid	**definition:** a diagram of the loss of useful energy at each level in the food chain **context:** Using the **energy pyramid**, the student studied the loss of energy in the food chain.
limiting factor **lim**-it-ing **fak**-tər lim·it·ing fac·tor	**definition:** a part of the environment that controls the growth or survival of a population **context:** When a population becomes too large, food becomes a **limiting factor**.
mimicry **mim**-i-krē mim·i·cry	**definition:** an adaptation in which an animal is protected against predators by its resemblance to another, unpleasant animal **context:** The resemblance of the Viceroy butterfly to the Monarch butterfly is an example of **mimicry**.
mutualism **myōō**-chōō-ə-liz-əm mu·tu·a·lis·m	**definition:** a relationship between two kinds of organisms that benefits both **context:** Flowers and their pollinators are a common form of **mutualism**.
organism ôr-gə-niz-əm or·gan·ism	**definition:** a living thing **context:** Many **organisms** live together in a community.
parasitism **par**-ə-sī-tiz-əm par·a·si·tis·m	**definition:** a relationship in which one organism lives in or on another organism and benefits from that relationship while the other organism may be harmed by it **context:** A tick attached to a dog is an example of **parasitism**.
pioneer community pī-ə-**nîr** kə-**myōō**-ni-tē pi·o·neer com·mu·ni·ty	**definition:** the first organisms to live in a once lifeless area **context:** In a newly formed volcanic island, the **pioneer community** is made up of bacteria, fungi, and algae.
pioneer species pī-ə-**nîr** spē-shēz pi·o·neer spe·cies	**definition:** the first species living in an otherwise lifeless area **context:** Mosses and lichens are **pioneer species**.
population pop-yə-**lā**-shən pop·u·la·tion	**definition:** the members of one species in an area **context:** The deer living in a pine forest are members of a **population**.
symbiosis sim-bē-**ō**-sis sym·bi·o·sis	**definition:** a relationship between two kinds of organisms that lasts over time **context:** The Nile crocodile opening its mouth to permit the Egyptian plover to feed on any leeches attached to its gums is an example of **symbiosis**.

Section 3.5: Vocabulary Building Activities

Symbiosis: Ecosystems are very delicate and must maintain a natural balance. Organisms maintain the natural balance through symbiosis. Copy and complete the table in your science journal.

Type of Symbiosis	Definition	Illustration
mutualism		
commensalism		
parasitism		

Hangman: Use the ecology vocabulary words to play HANGMAN with a partner. Write the letters of the alphabet at the bottom of a piece of paper. Think of a word, and then write the number of dashes that equal the number of letters in the word on your paper.

Example: If the word you chose is MIMICRY, write _ _ _ _ _ _ _ .

Your partner then tries to guess the word by naming letters. If the letter guessed is correct, fill in the corresponding dash with the letter. If the guess is incorrect, add a body part to the hangman, starting with a head. The "guesser" gets six tries (head, body, 2 arms, and 2 legs). As your partner guesses letters, cross them off the alphabet, so the letter won't be used again. If your partner guesses the word before the hangman is competed, they win. Start the next round.

WORD: _ _ _ _ _ _ _

A B C D E F G H I J K L M
N O P Q R S T U V W X Y Z

Online Resource: This award-winning website offers information about the environment through interactive, fun, and educational games and activities.
"EcoKids: Games and Activities." Earth Day Canada. <http://www.ecokidsonline.com/pub/games_activities/index.cfm>

Mimicry: Some organisms mimic the defenses of other organisms to fool their predators. Both the sand wasp and the yellow jacket can sting. Because they look alike, a predator that avoids one will avoid the other. Copy and complete the table below in your science journal. Name two organisms and describe the mimicry they use to fool their prey.

Organism	Mimicry
1.	
2.	

***Exxon Valdez* Oil Spill:** Research the 1989 *Exxon Valdez* oil spill off the Alaskan coast. What methods were used to clean up the shoreline and animals? What affect did the oil spill have on the marine ecosystem? Record the answers in your science journal.

Newspaper: Gather newspaper and magazine articles featuring environmental issues locally, nationally, and globally. Highlight words from your vocabulary list that appear in the articles. Create a classroom bulletin board to display the information.

Section 3.5: Vocabulary Building Activities (cont.)

Biotic and Abiotic Factors: An environment consists of two parts. The biotic part consists of all the organisms living in the environment. The abiotic part includes the non-living factors such as water, soil, light, and temperature. Copy and complete the table below in your science journal. Add two biotic and abiotic factors for each ecosystem.

Ecosystem	Biotic Factor	Abiotic Factor
prairie		
deciduous forest		
lake		

Adaptations: Name a predator, its prey, and the adaptation it uses to catch the prey. Name a prey, its predator, and the adaptation it uses to evade the predator. Record the answers in your science journal.

Environmental Organization: Ecologists organize the environment into five levels. Copy and complete the flow chart in your science journal. Add the correct definition for each level.

Biosphere

↑

Ecosystem

↑

Community

↑

Population

↑

Organism
a living thing

Energy Pyramids: The loss of energy at each level of the food chain can be illustrated using an energy pyramid. There are a larger number of organisms at the base. There are a decreasing number of organisms at each level of the pyramid. Green plants and other producers absorb the sun's energy and make food. The food they do not use is stored. The stored energy can be traced through the food chain to other organisms. When animals eat plants and animals, the stored energy in those organisms is passed along to the consumer. Some energy is lost as heat; the rest is used for growth and reproduction. This happens all the way up the food chain. The amount of available energy at each level decreases, limiting the number of organisms that can survive at each level. Draw an energy pyramid for an ecosystem in your science journal.

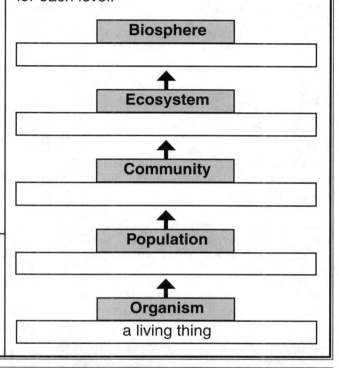

Section 4.1: Geology Word List

aquifer **ak**-wi-fər aq·ui·fer	**definition:** an underground body of water **context:** Sixty-five percent of the water used to grow crops comes from underground **aquifers**.
chemical weathering **kem**-i-kəl **weth**-ər-ing chem·i·cal weath·er·ing	**definition:** the wearing away of rock by oxidation or dissolving by acid **context: Chemical weathering** in caves causes stalactites and stalagmites.
crystal **kris**-təl crys·tal	**definition:** solids composed of atoms arranged in an orderly pattern **context:** Minerals possess one of six **crystal** shapes.
earthquake **ûrth**-kwāk earth·quake	**definition:** the movement of the earth's surface caused by waves of energy released as rocks move along faults in the crust **context:** An **earthquake** can cause buildings to collapse.
epicenter **ep**-i-sen-tər ep·i·cen·ter	**definition:** the spot on the earth's surface that is above the focus of an earthquake **context:** The earthquake is strongest at its **epicenter** directly above the focus where the earthquake occurred.
erosion i-**rō**-zhən e·ro·sion	**definition:** the wearing away of the earth's surface by wind, water, ice, or gravity **context:** Planting trees and grasses slows **erosion**.
fault **fôlt** fault	**definition:** a crack in the earth's crust where rocks rub against each other, releasing energy waves during an earthquake **context:** Earthquakes occur around a **fault**.
fold **fōld** fold	**definition:** a bend in a layer of rock caused by stress deep in the earth **context:** When rocks are under stress, they may fracture, fault, or **fold**.
fossil **fos**-əl fos·sil	**definition:** the remains of ancient, once-living organisms preserved in rock **context: Fossils** contain clues to the past.
fracture **frak**-chər frac·ture	**definition:** the tendency of a mineral or rock to break in a certain shape **context:** Some minerals **fracture** with rough or jagged edges.
freshwater **fresh**-wôt-ər fresh·wat·er	**definition:** the water that is not salt water **context:** Three percent of earth's water is **freshwater**.
groundwater **ground**-wôt-ər ground·wat·er	**definition:** the water beneath the surface of the earth between saturated soil and rock that supplies wells or springs **context: Groundwater** spread around the planet represents less than one percent of Earth's total water supply.
igneous rock **ig**-nē-əs **rok** ig·ne·ous rock	**definition:** the rocks formed by the crystallization of magma **context: Igneous rocks**, like obsidian, form when magma cools.

Section 4.1: Geology Word List (cont.)

mechanical weathering mi-**kan**-i-kəl w**e**th-ər-ing me·chan·i·cal weath·er·ing	**definition:** the physical forces that break rock **context: Mechanical weathering** can be seen when expanding ice breaks a rock into smaller pieces.
metamorphic rock met-ə-**môr**-fik rok met·a·mor·phic rock	**definition:** the rocks formed when sedimentary or igneous rocks undergo a change due to pressure or heat in the earth **context: Metamorphic rocks** are found deep in the earth.
mineral **min**-ər-əl min·er·al	**definition:** a solid, inorganic crystalline substance with a definite chemical composition **context:** All **minerals** share five characteristics.
Mohs' scale Mōz skāl Mohs scale	**definition:** a list of minerals of varying hardness **context:** The hardness of the mineral topaz can be measured using the **Mohs' scale**.
Pangaea pan-**jē**-ə Pan·gae·a	**definition:** the name of the landmass believed to have broken up into today's continents **context:** Scientists think that the continents were once joined together in one supercontinent, **Pangaea**.
Richter scale **rik**-tər sk**ā**l Rich·ter scale	**definition:** a scale used to describe how much energy is released by an earthquake **context:** In 1923, an earthquake measuring 8.3 on the **Richter scale** occurred in Tokyo, Japan.
rock cycle rok s**ī**-kəl rock cycle	**definition:** an explanation of how rocks change in a continuous cycle from igneous, to sedimentary, to metamorphic **context:** A diagram is used to explain the **rock cycle**.
sedimentary rock sed-ə-**men**-tə-rē rok sed·i·men·ta·ry rock	**definition:** the rocks formed from sediments (sand, clay, and other materials that settle in water) **context:** Sandstone is an example of a **sedimentary rock**.
seismograph s**ī**z-mə-graf seis·mo·graph	**definition:** an instrument that records earthquake waves **context:** Seismologists use **seismographs** to determine an earthquake's magnitude.
soil soil soil	**definition:** a mixture of crushed rock and pieces of organic material from plants and animals **context:** Fertile **soil** helps plants grow.
tectonic plates tek-**ton**-ik pl**ā**ts tec·ton·ic plates	**definition:** the pieces that compose the surface of the earth **context:** The crust has fractured into seven major **tectonic plates** that sometimes collide and grind past each other.
tsunami tsōō-**nä**-mē tsu·na·mi	**definition:** a large ocean wave, reaching up to 30 meters, caused by an underwater earthquake or landslide **context:** The United States developed the **Tsunami** Warning System in 1948.
volcano vol-**kā**-nō vol·ca·no	**definition:** a place in the earth's surface where hot magma is forced up, forming a mountain that erupts and builds upward **context:** Hawaii's Kilauea **volcano** is an active volcano.

Section 4.1: Vocabulary Building Activities

World Map: Keep track of earthquakes and volcanoes that occur throughout the world for a year on a world map. Check the newspapers or the Internet each day. Place push pins of one color at sites of earthquakes and push pins of another color at sites of active volcanoes. Which parts of the world seem most geologically active?

Online Resource: Learn more about earthquakes at the following animated website. "Earthquake for Kids." U.S. Department of the Interior. <http://earthquake.usgs.gov/learning/kid//>

Rocks: There are three main types of rocks—igneous, sedimentary, and metamorphic. Copy and complete the data table in your science journal.

Rock	How Formed	Example
1. sedimentary		
2. igneous		
3. metamorphic		

Minerals: Name four physical properties used to identify minerals. Record your answers in your science journal.

Faults: Faults are places where rocks break and then slide against one another—usually either up and down or side to side. Copy and complete the data table below in your science journal.

Fault	Name	Definition
1.		
2.		
3.		

Crossword Puzzle: Choose 12 vocabulary words to use for your puzzle. Select one of the words. On 1 cm grid paper, write one letter in each box forming your word horizontally (across) on the paper. Write the word lightly in pencil. Write another word vertically (down) on the grid paper so the words overlap where they have a common letter. Continue adding words to your puzzle until you have used all 12 words. Starting with 1, assign a number to each horizontal word and then the vertical words. At the bottom of the grid paper, write a definition for each of the words. Organize the definitions into "Across" and "Down" columns using the numbers on the puzzle grid. Trace around the squares you used with a marker. Erase the letters in each square. Trade your puzzle with a partner and solve.

Section 4.2: Oceanography Word List

abyssal plain ə-**bis**-əl **plān** a·byss·al plain	**definition:** a flat part of the ocean floor **context:** The **abyssal plain** is the flat part of the ocean floor.
Aqua-Lung **ak**-wə-lung aq·ua·lung	**definition:** an air tank worn by a diver **context:** The **Aqua-Lung** allowed the diver to explore the coral reef.
breaker **brāk**-ər break·er	**definition:** a wave in which the crest has tumbled forward **context:** The **breaker** tumbled toward the shore.
continental shelf kon-tə-**nen**-təl **shelf** con·ti·nen·tal shelf	**definition:** the part of the ocean bottom near land **context:** The **continental shelf** is the shallowest part of the ocean.
continental slope kon-tə-**nen**-təl **slōpe** con·ti·nen·tal slope	**definition:** the part of the ocean bottom where the continental shelf plunges downward sharply **context:** The **continental slope** plunges to the ocean floor.
coral reef **kôr**-əl **rēf** cor·al reef	**definition:** a large underwater formation created from the skeletons of colonies of tiny coral animals **context: Coral reefs** shelter the land from harsh ocean storms and floods, provide resources for fisheries, and attract millions of tourists every year.
currents **kûr**-ənts cur·rents	**definition:** the movement of water in a certain direction **context:** Underwater **currents** of the ocean are caused by the sun heating the ocean water.
desalination dē-**sal**-ə-nā-shən de·sal·i·na·tion	**definition:** the removal of salt from ocean water **context:** Key West, Florida, has a **desalination** plant to help provide the area with fresh water.
echo sounder ek-ō **soun**-dər ech·o soun·der	**definition:** a device that uses sonar (sound waves) to measure the depth of surface water bodies **context:** Scientists used an **echo sounder** to map the ocean floor.
marine mə-**rēn** ma·rine	**definition:** relating to the ocean **context:** A **marine** biologist is interested in ocean food chains.
mid-ocean ridge mid-ō-shən **rij** mid-ocean ridge	**definition:** a mountain chain on the ocean floor **context:** A **mid-ocean ridge** runs through every ocean on the earth.
ocean **ō**-shən o·cean	**definition:** the salt water covering approximately 75 percent of the earth's surface **context:** Shorelines are constantly changing because of the **ocean's** waves, tides, and currents.
ocean floor **ō**-shən **flôr** o·cean floor	**definition:** the part of the ocean that lies at the bottom of the continental slope **context:** Undiscovered life forms live on the **ocean floor**.

Section 4.2: Oceanography Word List (cont.)

plankton **plangk**-tən plank·ton	**definition:** the tiny plants and animals living on the ocean surface that can not be seen with the naked eye **context:** Some whales eat **plankton**.
prevailing winds pri-**vāl**-ing **winds** pre·vail·ing winds	**definition:** the winds that blow mostly from one direction **context: Prevailing winds** effect the surface currents of the oceans.
saline sā-lēn sa·line	**definition:** a saltwater solution **context:** Anyone who has accidentally swallowed ocean water knows that it is salty, or **saline**.
sand **sand** sand	**definition:** rock and mineral particles smaller than 2 mm in diameter **context:** Ocean shorelines are made of **sand**.
sand dune **sand dōōn** sand dune	**definition:** a hill of sand built up by wind **context:** Some of the world's largest **sand dunes** are located along the Oregon coast.
shoreline **shôr**-līn shore·line	**definition:** the land along the edge of the ocean water **context:** Canada's **shoreline** is the longest in the world because the country borders the ocean for thousands of miles.
sonar sō-**när** so·nar	**definition:** a method of detecting objects using sound waves **context:** With the invention of **sonar** equipment, the deepest areas of the ocean have been mapped.
submarine canyon **sub**-mə-rēn **kan**-yən sub·ma·rine can·yon	**definition:** a groove cut in the continental shelf and slope **context:** A **submarine canyon** is formed when sediment slides down the continental shelf and slope, making a deep groove.
tide tīd tide	**definition:** the rise and fall of ocean water **context:** The ocean **tides** are caused by the gravitational pull of the moon on the earth.
trade winds **trād winds** trade winds	**definition:** the winds that blow from east to west toward the equator **context:** Ships heading west try to sail in the area where the **trade winds** blow.
trench **trench** trench	**definition:** a deep ocean valley **context:** A **trench** is one of the deepest places in the ocean.
tsunami tsōō-**nä**-mē tsu·na·mi	**definition:** a large ocean wave, reaching up to 30 meters, caused by an underwater earthquake or landslide **context:** The **tsunami** wiped out several villages along the coast.
wave wāv wave	**definition:** the rise and fall movement of ocean water **context:** Forces such as the wind, earthquakes, and ships traveling on the ocean can cause a **wave**.
westerlies wes-tər-lēz wes·ter·lies	**definition:** the winds that blow from west to east away from the equator **context:** In the United States, storms move from west to east because of the **westerlies**.

Section 4.2: Vocabulary Building Activities

Ocean Currents: The temperature of ocean currents directly affects the temperature of the air above them. In general, warm ocean currents flow away from the equator, and cool currents flow toward the equator. Identify each current and record the answer in your science journal.

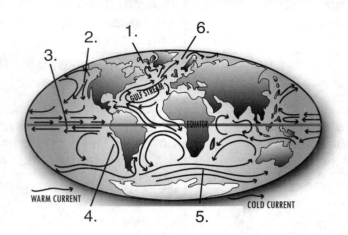

Ocean Water: Ocean water is salty, or saline. Salt affects some of the physical properties of water, especially density. It is much easier to float in water with a high salt content. The dissolved ions give water a greater weight per volume, which is the measure of density.

Activity

Mix two tablespoons of salt in a beaker of water until dissolved. Add 4 drops of food coloring. Slowly pour the salty water into a larger beaker partly filled with freshwater. What happens to the salty water? Explain. Record the answer in your science journal.

Online Resource: Create your own wave at the following interactive website. "Savage Sea Animation." Public Broadcasting Service.
<http://www.pbs.org/wnet/savageseas/multimedia/wavemachine.html>

Sand Dunes: Sand dunes act as a buffer zone, protecting the land behind them from the force of ocean wind and waves.

Pour a pile of dry sand on the bottom of a large box cut away as shown in the diagram. Place an electric fan facing the box. Turn the fan on low. Observe how the particles are moved. Next, turn the fan on high. What happens when the velocity of the wind is increased? Record the answers in your science journal.

Sonar: Oceanographers, people who study the ocean, use sonar to track objects underwater. Sonar is a device that uses sound waves sent out by objects to detect and locate objects underwater. Complete the following activity to see how sonar reflects sound waves from objects underwater.

Activity

Put a clear glass pie plate onto an overhead projector. Pour water into the plate. Turn the projector on. The image of the water will be projected onto the screen. Fill an eyedropper with water. Hold the dropper 6 inches above the pie plate. Drop several drops of water into the middle of the plate of water. Record what happens in your science journal.

Section 4.3: Meteorology Word List

air mass âr mas air mass	**definition:** a large region of the atmosphere where the air has similar temperature and humidity throughout **context:** Weather is affected by six major **air masses**.
air pressure âr presh-ər air pres·sure	**definition:** the weight of air **context:** **Air pressure** is also known as atmospheric pressure.
atmosphere at-mə-sfîr at·mo·sphere	**definition:** the blanket of gases that surrounds Earth **context:** The sun and its interaction with earth's **atmosphere** is the driving force for our weather.
climate klī-mit cli·mate	**definition:** the average weather pattern of a region **context:** Polar, temperate, and tropical are the earth's three **climate** zones.
convection current kən-vek-shən kûr-ənt con·vec·tion cur·rent	**definition:** a current's movement in fluids caused by heat **context:** **Convection currents** carry heat energy in churning cells of moving air.
Coriolis effect kôr-ē-ō-lis i-fekt Cor·i·o·lis ef·fect	**definition:** the deflection of winds caused by the rotation of the earth on its axis **context:** The **Coriolis effect**, along with the flow of air caused by differences in heating, causes distinct wind patterns.
dew point dōō pôint dew point	**definition:** the temperature at which the moisture in the air begins or would begin to condense **context:** Warm air can hold more water, so the humidity must be higher during warm weather to reach the **dew point**.
El Niño el nēn-yō El Ni·ño	**definition:** a change in climate that occurs when trade winds weaken west of Peru and whose effects can be felt worldwide **context:** During **El Niño**, water temperature rises, increasing the chances of stormy weather.
forecast fôr-kast fore·cast	**definition:** a prediction about future weather based on meteorological observations **context:** Weather satellites help meteorologists **forecast** weather.
front frunt front	**definition:** a boundary between air masses with different temperatures **context:** A **front** is where active weather occurs.
global warming glō-bəl wôrm-ing glo·bal warm·ing	**definition:** the rise in the earth's temperatures due to an increased greenhouse effect **context:** An increase in greenhouse gases is one reason for **global warming**.
greenhouse effect grēn-hous i-fekt green·house ef·fect	**definition:** the natural heating caused by atmospheric gases trapping heat at the earth's surface **context:** Without the **greenhouse effect**, Earth would be cold and lifeless.

Section 4.3: Meteorology Word List (cont.)

humidity hyo͞o-**mid**-i-tē hu·mid·i·ty	**definition:** the moisture in the air **context:** Meteorologists read relative **humidity** with a psychrometer.
hurricane **hûr**-i-kān hur·ri·cane	**definition:** a tropical cyclone with wind speeds of at least 74 mph or more **context: Hurricanes** are powerful storms formed over warm water.
hydrologic cycle hī-drə-**läj**-ik **sī**-kəl hy·dro·log·ic cy·cle	**definition:** the exchange of water between land, bodies of water, and the atmosphere; also known as the water cycle **context: Hydrologic cycle** is another name for water cycle.
insolation in-sō-**lā**-shən in·so·la·tion	**definition:** the radiant energy from the sun received by the earth **context: Insolation** is affected by the angle at which the sun's rays strike the earth.
jet stream **jet strēm** jet stream	**definition:** the narrow wind belts found near the top of the troposphere **context: Jet streams** have a major effect on our weather.
latent heat **lā**-tənt **hēt** la·tent heat	**definition:** the energy stored when evaporation turns a liquid into a gas **context:** During condensation, **latent heat** is released.
meteorology mē-tē-ə-**räl**-ə-jē me·te·o·rol·o·gy	**definition:** the study of weather **context: Meteorology** deals with understanding the forces and causes of weather.
radiation rā-dē-**ā**-shən ra·di·a·tion	**definition:** the transfer of energy by electromagnetic waves **context:** The sun's **radiation** causes water to change into water vapor.
relative humidity **rel**-ə-tiv hyo͞o-**mid**-i-tē rel·a·tive hu·mid·i·ty	**definition:** the amount of moisture in a given amount of air relative to what could be contained if the given amount of air were completely saturated **context:** It it important to know the **relative humidity** when watching for precipitation.
saturated sach-ə-rā-tid sat·u·ra·ted	**definition:** the point where no more liquid can be absorbed, dissolved, or retained **context:** Air **saturated** with water vapor has a relative humidity of 100 percent.
thunderstorm **thən**-dər-stôrm thun·der·storm	**definition:** a weather condition where lightning and thunder are present **context: Thunderstorms** form inside warm, moist air masses and at fronts.
tornado tôr-**nā**-dō tor·na·do	**definition:** a violent, whirling wind that moves across the ground in a narrow path **context:** A **tornado** forms in low cumulonimbus clouds.
weather we*th*-ər weath·er	**definition:** the conditions of the lower atmosphere from day to day at any given place and time **context:** Because it holds a layer of gases, or atmosphere, close around itself, Earth experiences **weather**.

Section 4.3: Vocabulary Building Activities

Atmosphere: The earth is surrounded by different layers of air called the atmosphere. Weather occurs in the earth's atmosphere. Copy and complete the data table below in your science journal.

Layer	Characteristics
1. Troposphere	
2. Stratosphere	
3. Mesosphere	
4. Thermosphere	
5. Ozonosphere	
6. Ionosphere	
7. Exosphere	
8. Magnetosphere	

Hydrologic Cycle: The water cycle has three parts: evaporation, condensation, and precipitation. Identify each part of the water cycle in the diagram. Record the answers in your science journal.

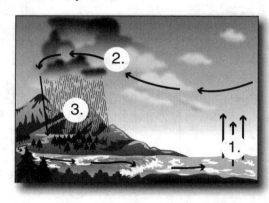

Severe Weather: Each year tornadoes and hurricanes cause millions of dollars of damage. Explain the difference in these two destructive storms. Copy and complete the data table below in your science journal.

Storm	How the Storm Forms	Description	Types of Damage
1. tornado			
2. hurricane			

Dew Point: Put some ice and water into a tin can. Place a thermometer in the can. (Do not stir the mixture with the thermometer.) When water droplets form on the outside of the can, measure the temperature of the ice/water mixture. This temperature is the dew point. Dew is formed when water vapor in the air changes to drops by coming in contact with the cold air.

Online Resource: Up-to-date weather information can be found at the following website. "National Weather Service." National Oceanic and Atmospheric Administration's <http://www.nws.noaa.gov/>

Weather vs. Climate: Read each statement and decide if weather or climate is being described. Record the answers in your science journal.

1. Summers in Missouri are warm and humid.
2. Stratus clouds presently cover the entire sky.
3. Our lowest temperature last winter was -9°C.
4. The air temperature outside is 60°C.
5. April is our rainiest month.
6. The highest temperature ever recorded in Chicago, Illinois, was 44°C on July 10, 1936.
7. Snow is falling at the rate of 6 cm per hour.
8. The average temperature for the month of January is -3°C in Denver, Colorado.

Section 4.4: Astronomy Word List

asteroid **as**-tə-roid as·te·roid	**definition:** the irregular-shaped rocks, smaller than planets, that revolve around the sun **context:** An **asteroid** is too small to be a planet.
asteroid belt **as**-tə-roid **belt** as·te·roid belt	**definition:** the concentration of asteroids between Mars and Jupiter **context:** The **asteroid belt** separates the inner planets from the outer planets in our solar system.
astronomical unit as-trə-**nom**-i-kəl **yoo**-nit as·tro·nom·i·cal u·nit	**definition:** the average distance from Earth to the sun; approximately 93 million miles (150 million kilometers) **context:** AU is the abbreviation for **astronomical unit.**
astronomy ə-**stron**-ə-mē a·stron·o·my	**definition:** the study of celestial bodies that include the stars, planets, and comets **context:** Studying **astronomy** gives scientists a better understanding of Earth's origin.
comet **kom**-it com·et	**definition:** a combination of ice, dust, and rock material that moves in an orbit around the sun **context:** A **comet** has a head and a long, flowing, vapor tail.
constellation kon-stə-**lā**-shən con·stel·la·tion	**definition:** the star groups that resemble familiar objects or characters **context:** The Big and Little Dippers are **constellations.**
eclipse i-**klips** e·clipse	**definition:** the blocking of light from one object by another **context:** A solar or lunar **eclipse** can be seen from Earth.
ellipse i-**lips** el·lipse	**definition:** an oval shape **context:** The orbits of the planets are not circular but resemble an elongated circle called an **ellipse.**
galaxy **gal**-ək-sē gal·ax·y	**definition:** a group of billions of stars **context:** **Galaxies**, such as the Milky Way, have different shapes.
gravity **grav**-i-tē grav·i·ty	**definition:** the force that keeps planets in orbit around the sun and governs the rest of the motion in the solar system **context:** **Gravity** alone holds us to the earth's surface and explains the phenomenon of tides.
light-year **līt**-yîr light-year	**definition:** a unit of length equal to the distance that light can travel in one year in a vacuum; approximately 5.88 trillion miles (9.46 trillion kilometers) **context:** A **light-year** equals the distance that light can travel in one year.
meteor **mē**-tē-ôr me·te·or	**definition:** a meteoroid (space rock or dust from a comet or a broken up asteroid) that burns up in the atmosphere **context:** Shooting stars are actually **meteors.**
meteorite **mē**-tē-ə-rīt me·te·o·rite	**definition:** a meteoroid that hits the earth's surface **context:** **Meteorites** are believed to be debris from asteroid collisions.

Section 4.4: Astronomy Word List (cont.)

meteoroid mē-tē-ə-roid me·te·or·oid	**definition:** the space rock or dust from a comet or broken-up asteroid **context:** Many **meteoroids** enter Earth's atmosphere each year.
meteor shower mē-tē-ôr **shou**-ər me·te·or show·er	**definition:** an event where a large number of meteoroids burn up as they enter Earth's atmosphere **context:** The Leonids, a spectacular **meteor shower**, can be seen each November.
moon mo͞on moon	**definition:** a celestial body that revolves around a planet **context:** Earth's **moon** has a barren, rocky surface.
orbit ôr-bit or·bit	**definition:** the path the moon, planets, asteroids, and comets follow as they travel around the sun **context:** Earth's **orbit** around the sun is an oval shape.
orbital plane ôr-bit-əl **plān** or·bit·al plane	**definition:** the imaginary surface that contains an object's path **context:** The **orbital plane**, expanding outward from the sun's equator, includes Earth and most of the planets in our solar system.
planet **plan**-it plan·et	**definition:** an object bigger than an asteroid orbiting a star **context:** **Planets** travel in elliptical orbits around the sun.
revolution rev-ə-**lo͞o**-shən rev·o·lu·tion	**definition:** the orbit of a planet around the sun or a satellite around a planet **context:** Earth makes one **revolution** about the sun in a year.
rotation rō-**tā**-shən ro·ta·tion	**definition:** the spinning of an object **context:** Earth makes a complete **rotation** on its axis every 24 hours.
satellite sat-l-īt sat·el·lite	**definition:** a small body that orbits around a larger body **context:** The moon is Earth's natural **satellite**.
solar system sō-lər **sis**-təm so·lar sys·tem	**definition:** the sun and all the objects revolving around the sun **context:** There are eight planets in our **solar system**.
star **stär** star	**definition:** a distant sun glowing from heat produced by nuclear reactions at its center **context:** Planets are closer to Earth than other **stars** are.
sun sun sun	**definition:** a star; the star at the center of our solar system **context:** The **sun** is a star made of gases so hot they glow, giving off light.
terrestrial planet tə-res-trē-əl **plan**-it ter·res·tri·al plan·et	**definition:** the inner planets Mercury, Venus, Earth, and Mars **context:** Mercury, Venus, Earth, and Mars are **terrestrial planets** that have solid, rocky surfaces.
universe yo͞o-nə-vûrs u·ni·verse	**definition:** the planets, sun, moons, stars, and everything that exist in space **context:** The **universe** is endless.

Section 4.4: Vocabulary Building Activities

Ellipse: Planetary orbits are not circular but resemble an elongated circle called an ellipse.

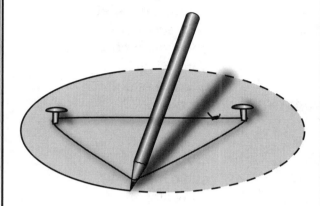

How to Draw an Ellipse
Place a sheet of cardboard under a page in your science journal. Push two thumb tacks into the middle of the paper 2 inches apart. Tie the two ends of an 8-inch-long string together to make a loop. Place the loop around the tacks. Pull the loop of string tight with a pencil. Draw an ellipse as you move the pencil around the pins on the paper.

Phases of the Moon: The diagram below shows the phases of the moon. Identify each phase and record the answers in your science journal.

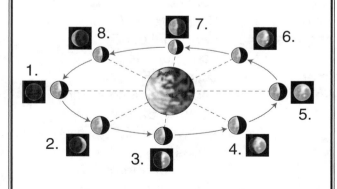

Online Resource: Learn more about the orbital motions of the planets, asteroids, and comets in our solar system at the following animated website.
"Solar System Visualize." University of Maryland. <http://janus.astro.umd.edu/SolarSystems/>

Planets: Record the answers to the questions below in your science journal.

1. In the diagram, number 1 represents Mercury and number 3 represents Earth. Which planet is represented by the number 2?

2. In the diagram, number 1 represents Saturn and number 3 represents Neptune. Which planet is represented by the number 2?

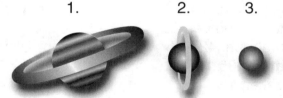

3. In the diagram, number 1 represents Earth and number 3 represents Jupiter. Which planet is represented by the number 2?

Index

Index (cont.)

Index (cont.)

Index (cont.)

More Science Words

absorption	cloud	fish
acid	cocoon	flood
acid rain	cold-blooded	focus
adult	coma	fog
algae	concave	food chain
alkaline	condensation	food web
alternating current	coniferous forest	frog
amino acid	coniferous tree	fulcrum
amoeba	consumer	gamma ray
amphibian	convex	gas
anemometer	core	gem
animal	corona	gemstone
antenna	cosmos	gills
arachnid	cotyledon	glucose
arthropod	crater	grassland
asthenosphere	crust	habitat
astronaut	crustacean	hail
aurora	cumulonimbus	hemisphere
autumn	cumulus	herbivore
autumnal equinox	day	hibernation
axis	deciduous forest	horizon
bacteria	deciduous tree	host
balance scale	decomposer	humus
barometer	deposit	impact
biochemical rock	deposition	inclined plane
biome	desert	infrared ray
bird	dicot	inner core
black hole	direct current	intrusive
blizzard	dissolve	Jupiter
boulder	droplet	kingdom
carbon dioxide	dwarf star	larva
carnivore	Earth	law
cartilage	echinoderms	leaf
caterpillar	endangered species	lever
celestial	environment	liquid
celestial sphere	epicenter	lunar eclipse
cell	equinox	magma
cell membrane	euglena	magnifying glass
characteristic	extinct	magnitude
chemical change	extrasolar planet	mammal
chrysalis	extrusive	mantle
cirrus	fall	mare
clay	feather	Mars

More Science Words (cont.)

marsupial
meander
mechanical energy
Mercury
microscopic
migration
Milky Way Galaxy
mixture
mollusk
monocot
motion
NASA
nebulae
Neptune
neutral
niche
night
nova
nymph
omnivore
ore
outer core
oxygen
oxidation
paleontologist
paramecium
pebble
penumbra
phase
phloem
photosphere
physical change
pistil
planetarium
Polaris
poles
pollen
precipitation
predator
pressure
prey
producer
protozoa

pulley
pulsar
pupa
qualitative
quantitative
quasar
rain
rain gauge
reproduce
reptile
ring
Ring of Fire
rock
root
runoff
sand
Saturn
scavenger
screw
season
sediment
shadow
shooting star
silt
skeleton
sky
sleet
smog
snow
solar eclipse
solar flare
solid
solstice
space
spacecraft
species
spring
stamen
stem
stomata
stratus
sunspot
tadpole

taiga
telescope
theory
transmission
tropical rain forest
tundra
umbra
Ursa Major
Venus
virus
visible light
warm-blooded
water cycle
water vapor
watt
weathering
wedge
wheel and axle
wind vane
winter
winter solstice
X-ray
xylem
year

Answer Keys

Chapter 1—Scientific Inquiry Vocabulary
Section 1.1: Scientific Method (page 8–9)
Scientific Method:
Research - gather information
Hypothesis - an educated guess of an answer to the question
Procedure - the experiment written and carefully followed step-by-step to test the hypothesis
Data - information collected during the experiment
Conclusion - statement of whether or not the results support the hypothesis

Variables:
Hypothesis #1 - Variable: brand of batteries; Control Group: type of flashlight, bulb, location of experiment
Hypothesis #2 - Variable: amount of fertilizer; Control Group: plants, soil, sunlight, when fertilized

Formulate a Conclusion:
Ever Last batteries operate a flashlight longer than Mighty Power and #1 Battery

The Big Question: Answers will vary.

Variables:
Independent Variable - time measured in minutes
Dependent Variable - height of candle measured in millimeters at regular intervals of time (for example, every five minutes)
Controlled Variables - use same type of candle, air-drafts

Steps in Scientific Method:
6, 2, 5, 4, 1, 3

Section 1.2: Scientific Equipment (page 13–15)
Flask:
When air molecules are heated, they move further apart, causing the balloon to expand. Air molecules move closer together when cooled, causing the balloon to deflate.

Bunsen Burner:
1. C. barrel   2. B. air ports   3. D. gas inlet
4. A. base   5. E. needle valve

Safety Eyewear:
cotton - gray, powdery
wool - black, shiny

Medicine Dropper:
1. Yes   2. Yes   3. Yes   4. Yes
5. No   6. No   7. Yes   8. No

Section 1.3: Scientific Measurement (page 18–19)
Practice Problems:
1. 0.006 L   2. 48,000 mL   3. 88,000 g
4. 0.108 kg   5. 120 mm   6. 1,400 cm
7. 6,250 mL   8. 950 cm

Chapter 2—Physical Science Vocabulary
Section 2.1: Matter (page 22)
Word Shape Puzzles:
1. electron   2. proton

Section 2.2: Chemistry (page 25)
Chemical Formula:
1. O_2 2. CO_2 3. NaCl   4. $CaCO_3$
5. KNO_3

Mixtures:
1. homogeneous   2. homogeneous
3. heterogeneous   4. heterogeneous
5. heterogeneous   6. heterogeneous

Chemical Bonds:
1. covalent, the chemical bond that forms between nonmetal atoms when they share electrons
2. ionic, the attraction between oppositely charged ions that hold them close together

Types of Mixtures: Examples will vary.
1. an evenly mixed mixture containing a solvent and at least one solute with the same properties
2. a mixture containing small, dissolved particles that do not settle out
3. a mixture in which the components are dispersed but large enough to see and to settle out

Solutions:
air - gas, gas, gas
ocean water - liquid, solid, liquid
cola drink - liquid, gas, liquid

Chemical Reactions:
1. endothermic   2. exothermic
3. exothermic   4. endothermic
5. exothermic   6. Answers will vary.
7. Answers will vary.

Section 2.3: Force and Motion (page 28)
Simple Machines:
1. third   2. second   3. first   4. third
5. second   6. third

Answer Keys (cont.)

Newton:
First - An object at rest tends to remain at rest, and an object in motion tends to continue moving in a straight line at a constant speed.
Second - A change in motion (speed or direction) of an object depends on the mass and force (push or pull) on the object.
Third - For every action, there is an equal and opposite reaction.

Motion:
1. 5 miles per hour   2. 60 kilometers per hour

Section 2.4: Energy (page 31)
Forms of Energy:
(Examples will vary.)
1. energy an object has because of its motion or position
2. energy related to the temperature of a substance
3. energy carried by light and other kinds of electromagnetic waves
4. energy produced by electric charges
5. energy stored in chemical bonds
6. energy contained in the nuclei of atoms

Resources:
1. nonrenewable   2. renewable   3. renewable
4. renewable (with proper management)
5. nonrenewable   6. nonrenewable

Heat Transfer:
1. radiation   2. conduction   3. convection

Section 2.5: Waves, Sound, and Light (page 34)
Light Waves:
1. absorption; all wavelengths of light are taken in and none are reflected
2. transmission; light is bent as it travels from the air through the glass
3. reflection; light bounces from the shiny surface

Waves:
1. height   2. crest   3. wavelength
4. trough   5. amplitude

Electromagnetic Spectrum:
Shortest - gamma rays
Longest - radio waves

Section 2.6: Electricity and Magnetism (page 37)
Venn Diagram:
Series - Only one path for current to flow
Parallel - Several paths for current to flow
Both - Unbroken path through which current flows

Electromagnet:
Add more wire, batteries, or nails

Circuits:
1. series   2. parallel
3. None of the lights will light.
4. The other lights will stay on.

Ohms: 12

Chapter 3—Life Science Vocabulary
Section 3.1: Structure of Life (page 40–41)
Plant and Animal Cells:
1. Golgi bodies   2. ribosome
3. endoplasmic reticulum   4. nucleus
5. cell membrane   6. vacuoles
7. cytoplasm   8. mitochondria
9. Golgi bodies   10. cell wall
11. chloroplast   12. endoplasmic reticulum
13. ribosome

Venn Diagram:
Plant - cell wall, chloroplasts
Animal - no cell wall, no chloroplasts
Both - nucleus, cytoplasm, cell membrane, Golgi bodies, mitochondria, vacuoles, ribosomes, endoplasmic reticulum
The cell wall is a rigid structure outside the cell membrane that gives the plant support. Animals either have a skeleton or an exoskeleton for support.

Diffusion:
1. The scent escaped through small holes in the rubber of the balloon.
2. The cell membrane has pores in it that allow molecules to go in and out of the cell.

Types of Cells:
eukaryotic cell - a single cell with a nucleus; most cells except bacteria
prokaryotic cell - the simplest type of cell that has no nucleus; DNA and other materials are scattered throughout the cytoplasm; bacteria and their relatives

Answer Keys (cont.)

Section 3.2: Classification (page 44)

Leaf Food Factory:
Diagram should include: light energy + carbon dioxide + water are used to make glucose in the chloroplast. Oxygen is released.

Vascular vs. Nonvascular:
vascular - plants with tube-like structures inside the plant used to carry food, water, and minerals
nonvascular - a plant that does not have stems and roots; does not have xylem and phloem tissue; include mosses, hornworts, liverworts

Venn Diagram:
Respiration - the process of converting stored food into usable energy; during the process water and carbon dioxide are released to the atmosphere; light is not needed
Transpiration - the loss of water through the leaf; stomata pulls water up through the plant from the roots; transpiration is the way plants use water to carry nutrients through their structure; occurs while there is sunlight
Both - major process of plant growth

Simple Organisms:
Monera - consists of organisms composed of prokaryotic cells; bacteria
Fungi (singular fungus) - a group of organisms that lack chlorophyll and obtain nutrients from dead or living organic matter; molds, rusts, mildews, mushrooms, and yeast
Protista - the kingdom that includes unicellular eukaryotic organisms that cannot be classified into any of the other eukaryotic kingdoms; protozoa and algae

Section 3.3: Life Cycles (page 47–48)

Vocabulary Code Puzzle:
1. exoskeleton   2. metamorphosis
3. insect   4. egg   5. flower

Venn Diagram:
Complete - the larva (immature insect) is very different from the adult, and a distinct pupa (cocoon) is formed.
Incomplete - the immature stage (or nymph) looks like the adult, no pupa stage
Both - molt, egg, larva, adult stages

Animal Life Cycles:
1. complete   2. incomplete   3. incomplete
4. simple   5. simple   6. ametabolous

Frog:
1. egg - Frogs lay their eggs in water or wet places.
2. tadpole - After 21 days, the embryo leaves its jelly shell and attaches itself to a weed in the water. This quickly becomes a tadpole, a baby frog. The tadpoles grow until they are big enough to break free into the water. They swim and have a tail. They eat algae. After about five weeks, the tadpole begins to change, grow legs, and become more frog-like. They eat plants and decaying animal matter.
3. adult - Eleven weeks after the egg was laid, a fully developed frog with lungs, legs, and no tail emerges from the water. This frog will live mostly on land, and occasionally swims. The tiny frogs begin to eat insects and worms.

Section 3.4: Reproduction and Heredity (page 51)

Inherited Traits vs. Acquired Traits:
1. acquired   2. inherited   3. inherited
4. acquired

Section 3.5: Ecology (page 54–55)

Symbiosis:
mutualism - a relationship between two kinds of organisms that benefits both
commensalism - a relationship between two kinds of organisms that benefits one without harming the other
parasitism - a relationship in which one organism lives in or on another organism and benefits from that relationship while the other organism may be harmed by it

Exxon Valdez Oil Spill:
1. dumping a dispersant (chemical agent used to break up concentrations of oil), there was not enough wave action to mix the dispersant with the oil in the water
2. burning the oil spill
3. mechanical cleanup: booms and skimmers to skim the oil off the surface of the water
Thousands of animals died immediately. It destroyed the shoreline and ocean animal habitats.

Biotic and Abiotic Factors:
Answers will vary.

Environmental Organization:
Biosphere - the part of the Earth that supports life
Ecosystem - interaction of all the living and nonliving things in an environment
Community - organisms living in an area
Population - members of one species living in an area

Answer Keys (cont.)

Chapter 4—Earth and Space Science Vocabulary
Section 4.1: Geology (page 58)
Rocks:
1. created when layers of sediment settle to the bottom of the ocean and, over thousands of years, are pressed together; contains fossils; soft with layers; examples will vary but may include chalk, coal, sandstone, shale, and limestone
2. created when molten lava cools; glossy, crystalline, coarse-grained; examples will vary but may include granite, basalt, obsidian, pumice, and quartz
3. created when sedimentary or igneous rocks undergo a change due to pressure or heat within the earth; hard; crystals may appear; layers may develop; examples will vary but may include slate and marble

Faults:
1. normal fault - one in which the hanging wall falls down relative to the foot wall due to tensional stress
2. reverse fault - one in which the hanging wall moves up relative to the foot wall due to compression
3. thrust fault - the hanging wall is pushed up and then over the foot wall at a low angle

Section 4.2: Oceanography (page 61)
Ocean Currents:
1. Labrador Current
2. California Current
3. Equatorial Counter Current
4. Peru Current
5. Antarctic Circumpolar Current
6. North Atlantic Current

Ocean Water:
The salt water sinks because the salt gives the water greater weight.

Sand Dunes:
Answers will vary.

Sonar:
The drops of water falling into the plate create a wave that goes out from the middle of the plate and bounces back from the sides.

Section 4.3: Meteorology (page 64)
Atmosphere:
1. troposphere - most weather occurs here
2. stratosphere - ozone layer, jets fly here
3. mesosphere - protects earth from meteors, (shooting stars burn up here)
4. thermosphere - few molecules here
5. ozonosphere - protects the earth from sun's UV rays
6. ionosphere - radio waves bounce back to the earth's surface from here
7. exosphere - artificial satellites orbit here
8. magnetosphere - the earth's magnetic field, causes aurora borealis (Northern Lights)

Hydrologic Cycle:
1. evaporation   2. condensation
3. precipitation

Severe Weather:
1. formed during thunderstorms, winds blow at different heights and at different speeds causing a funnel cloud; violent whirling winds that move in a narrow path over land, winds spin as fast as 500 km per hour; destroy lives and property in seconds with violent winds
2. large, swirling, low-pressure systems that form over tropical oceans, begin when several small thunderstorms come together; when winds reach 120 km per hour, storm is called a hurricane; can destroy property and take lives with storm surge flooding and high winds

Weather vs. Climate:
1. climate   2. weather   3. weather
4. weather   5. climate   6. weather
7. weather   8. climate

Section 4.4: Astronomy (page 67)
Phases of the Moon:
1. new moon   2. waxing crescent moon
3. first quarter moon   4. waxing gibbous moon
5. full moon   6. waning gibbous moon
7. third quarter moon   8. waning crescent moon

Planets:
1. Venus   2. Uranus   3. Mars

Bibliography

Beaver, John B. and Barbara R. Sandall. *Simple Machines: Connecting Students to Science Series.* Quincy, Illinois: Mark Twain Media, Inc., 2002.

Curtis, Mary E. and Ann Marie Longo. November 2001. *Teaching Vocabulary to Adolescents to Improve Comprehension.* International Reading Association. <http://www.readingonline.org/articles/curtis/>

Logan, LaVerne. *Rocks and Minerals: Connecting Students to Science Series.* Quincy, Illinois: Mark Twain Media, Inc., 2002.

Logan, LaVerne. *Sound: Connecting Students to Science Series.* Quincy, Illinois: Mark Twain Media, Inc., 2002.

Beaver, John B. and Don Powers. *Electricity and Magnetism: Connecting Students to Science Series.* Quincy, Illinois: Mark Twain Media, Inc., 2003.

Marzano, Robert J. and Debra J. Pickering. *Building Academic Vocabulary: Teacher's Manual.* ASCD, 2005.

Marzano, Robert. *Building Background Knowledge for Academic Achievement: Research on What Works in Schools.* ASCD, 2004.

Merriam-Webster Online. 7 May 2008. <http://www.merriam-webster.com/dictionary/chromat->

Powers, Don and John B. Beaver. *The Solar System: Connecting Students to Science Series.* Quincy, Illinois: Mark Twain Media, Inc., 2004.

Project G.L.A.D. February 20, 2007. Orange County Department of Education. <http://www.projectglad.com/>

Raham, Gary. *Science Tutor: Earth and Space Science.* Quincy, Illinois: Mark Twain Media, Inc., 2006.

Raham, Gary. *Science Tutor: Life Science.* Quincy, Illinois: Mark Twain Media, Inc., 2006.

Sandall, Barbara R. *Chemistry: Connecting Students to Science Series.* Quincy, Illinois: Mark Twain Media, Inc., 2004.

Sandall, Barbara R. *Light and Color: Connecting Students to Science Series.* Quincy, Illinois: Mark Twain Media, Inc., 2004.

Sciencesaurus: A Student Handbook. Houghton Mifflin, 2002.

Science Vocabulary Strategies Handbook. 2007–2008. <www.pscubed.org/documents/CompleteBook.pdf>

Shireman, Myrl. *Physical Science.* Quincy, Illinois: Mark Twain Media, Inc., 1997.

78